Dearest _____ : This is a sacred invite to your tribe, so that together we may find and follow our Bliss.

(See full invitation on page 7)

A TRIBE CALLED BLISS

Break Through Superficial Friendships,
Create Real Connections,
Reach Your Highest Potential

LORI HARDER

G

GALLERY BOOKS

New York   London   Toronto   Sydney   New Delhi

Gallery Books

An Imprint of Simon & Schuster, Inc.

1230 Avenue of the Americas

New York, NY 10020

Note to readers: Certain names have been changed.

Copyright © 2018 by Lori Harder

This Gallery Books trade paperback edition May 2019

GALLERY BOOKS and colophon are trademarks of Simon & Schuster, Inc.

For information about special discounts for bulk purchases,
please contact Simon & Schuster Special Sales at 1-866-506-1949
or business@simonandschuster.com.

The Simon & Schuster Speakers Bureau can bring authors to your
live event. For more information, or to book an event, contact the
Simon & Schuster Speakers Bureau at 1-866-248-3049 or
visit our website at www.simonspeakers.com.

Interior design by Bryden Spevak

Manufactured in the United States of America

10 9 8 7 6 5 4 3 2 1

Library of Congress Cataloging-in-Publication Data is available.

ISBN 978-1-5011-7616-6
ISBN 978-1-5011-7617-3 (pbk)
ISBN 978-1-5011-7618-0 (ebook)

Behind every successful woman is a tribe of women who have her back.

This book is dedicated to all the women who have helped me on this journey.

CONTENTS

FOREWORD

By Gabrielle Bernstein

Four years ago I had a private coaching practice for a handful of people each year. I was very clear about the types of clients I wanted to work with—I wanted to help healers, teachers, and lightworkers amplify the platforms they'd already built. As the Universe would have it, I manifested my dream client. She was smart, successful, and totally committed to helping others. She led a tribe of empowered women to fulfill their highest purpose. This client was Lori Harder.

Lori's passion, dedication, and business savvy came through on our first call. What I loved most about coaching Lori was that she took my suggestions really seriously. She was ready to go big and willing to do whatever it took to grow her business and serve the world. Over the past four years I've had the privilege of watching Lori's visions become her reality. Her business has turned into a thriving enterprise and now includes a podcast that attracts millions of listeners. Every day she continues to grow her platform through speaking, workshops, and now her new book, *A Tribe Called Bliss*.

In this book, Lori offers a step-by-step guide to lifetime connection, sisterhood, and support. We can't do big work in the world without a little help! The pathway to success requires a community, and Lori is committed to helping others create one of their own. But these days finding a tribe can be very overwhelming because many of us live in less tightly knit communities and spend so much of our time online. It's easy to feel disconnected and separate from others. That's why Lori's book is so important. *A Tribe Called Bliss* will hook you up with the spiritually rooted friendships you long for and the support you need to live up to your highest potential.

Women need the support of a sisterhood now more than ever, and that is what this book encourages: sisterhood for all women. It's for women who are already leaders and change-makers in the world, as well as those who are still early in discovering their paths. *A Tribe Called Bliss* helps people live to their fullest, authentically connect to each other, and find their place in the world. And the benefits of having a tribe don't stop there.

Women who have strong social circles live longer, happier, healthier lives compared to those who lack supportive connections. To belong is one of our core desires as humans, and as women we need something uplifting and real to bond over and an accessible way to do it.

True connections are forged when women get vulnerable and share our stories and deep emotional experiences with other women. It's so important that we create safe, nurturing spaces in which we can do this. Without these connections, we miss out on what makes life so joyous.

In this book, Lori shows what her life looked like before she found her tribe. She then shows you how to tap into the bliss of everyday life and how to surround yourself with your very own tribe of high-vibe, loving, and like-minded souls. Lori's own tribe was founded on the agreements in this book, and she shares her structure so you can create yours. Not only will you learn how to cultivate your tribe, but Lori will also show you how to break free of limiting beliefs and tap into your higher power.

When we do spiritual work and embark on new journeys, we often run into problems like negative self-talk and old belief systems. Lori takes the knowledge she has gained over decades of helping thousands of women overcome their fears and shows you how to break free of your self-sabotaging behaviors so you can show up for yourself and your relationships.

And here's the beauty of this book: You don't have to do all the work on your own. You're meant to do a portion of the work WITH your tribe. Along with each chapter's lesson, there are self-work exercises for both you and the tribe you're looking to cultivate or for an already established circle.

Lori has structured this book as a tool to bring your tribe together, so you can immediately start reaping the benefits! You'll take more risks and leap out of your comfort zone knowing that women in your tribe are doing it with you. You'll celebrate each individual's wins like they are your own, because when one of you rises it elevates the entire group. When one of you cries, you'll welcome that emotion and acknowledge the pain.

Your tribe will help you see the beautiful lessons you've learned and remind you of your truth, your power, and your purpose. Embarking on that journey with your sisters and finding the joy in everything that comes your way is pure bliss.

A TRIBE
CALLED
BLISS

YOUR BLISS JOURNEY BEGINS HERE

Dearest Bliss-Tribe Sister,

I have been watching you. Not in a creeper way, but in the "I see you and I have been there" kind of way. I see the struggle, stress, loneliness, and fear you're feeling despite choosing to take steps to better yourself and build your dreams. Maybe you're like I was and pictured this journey to your "best life" being a lot more connected, fun, and fulfilling than your current reality of feeling totally uncertain or disconnected. Perhaps you identify more with anxiety than those said to be "following their bliss," because you're alone behind a screen, doing housework, grinding away on your business, taking care of family, and trying to be healthy. This might leave you questioning if you're going about this bliss thing the right way, or maybe it's the misconception or denial of your bliss that is actually causing all the pain?

Distractions and stress are ever increasing, but so is our desire to reach our highest potential and be happy. But what fun is it if we are not enjoying the journey and growing ourselves alone? Does this mean it's true that it's lonely at the top? Do you even want to reach bliss if no one else is there with you? Take a breath because I've got good news: You are not meant to do this alone and you don't have to. You are simply missing the tools, awareness, and words to be able to find your like-minded tribe, connect to them deeply, experience true bliss, and have some fun on the journey together.

One thing we know for sure is the old way of "being" and creating relationships is not working anymore. Texting, emailing, surface-level happy hours and bonding over gossip, judgment, drama, and grudges are leaving you feeling emptier than a candy dish at a Weight Watchers meeting. The suppression of who we really are in our relationships causes comparison and the side effects are shame and playing small. Our silent suffering and confinement of our need to deeply connect manifest in a thousand different ways that lead you to believe there is something "wrong" with you. Let me be clear, everything about you is more than right, but you are lacking a very necessary and vital piece of the puzzle. Tribe.

We are on this earth to create the type of experiences and life that forces the highest version of ourselves to show up. We are here to share love, use our gifts, and find the solutions to our own obstacles so we can then teach what we've learned and how we moved through it to others. We are here to expand into the extraordinary beings we are intended to be. We are not meant to move through this life alone but to find a tribe of loving and supportive sisters to come together and share our stories, extract our unique message, and use our voices. It will only be by sharing our strengths and struggles that we will break free and rise up to our highest potential and bliss. In isolation, our shame and fear grow stronger. Through vulnerable, compassionate union we free not only our souls and the souls closest to us, but we shift, heal, and elevate the soul of the planet.

This book you hold in your hands is not a book. It is your opportunity to create your own movement. A Tribe Called Bliss will lead you to find your like-minded tribe and show you how to love them hard. It is a step-by-step guide that literally provides everything you need to build your tribe, and it lays out exactly how to formulate and set up each tribe meeting after that. It even gives scripts of what to say and how to break the surface talk when you're at a loss for words! This book is the new way, the way of creating safe, sacred spaces and loving relationships that incite real, lasting sisterhood. You now have a map and a set of tools that will guide you through all that is holding you back from reaching your highest potential as a human being. Read on, and you will see how fast this book can work its magic. Before long you will be witnessing meaningful, spiritual connections with yourself and others, creating supportive circles of women, experiencing absolute clarity on your path, remarkable healing, and enduring inner peace.

This is your faith-drenched invitation to join my Bliss Tribe. And by picking up this book you've taken the initiative and anointed yourself ready to create your own Bliss Tribe movement. You see, a tribe can't exist without all of YOU, the leaders, a common interest, and a way to connect and interact. This book provides the agreements, scripts, topics, structure, and guidelines for you to get started and understand how to make your tribe work. Tribes live and die by the ability to stick to the agreements, equality, and respect of time and trust. Because tribes are only as strong as the people in them, this book also provides lessons on how to develop and work on your own personal growth at the same time as developing and learning with your tribe. Essentially you will be evolving and elevating yourself while profoundly uniting with your new tribe of sisters.

Don't be scared, this won't take much time and I know life is crazy enough. If you follow the directions in this book exactly, this new path will be a game changer and a bonus to all areas of your life. You will find you have more time and fulfillment despite adding this firm commitment, because you are about to make room for what actually gives you life. The last thing I want to do is add another to-do on the list. A Tribe Called Bliss will streamline your life and get you clear on what is and isn't a priority.

On this journey I will share everything that has worked for me to create a life and tribe that are beyond my wildest dreams so you can do the same. I also fully share what hasn't worked as well, and I hope you like to laugh, because we can't take ourselves too seriously on this journey. After all, this is meant to be fun!

Grab my hand (or you can just high-five this book) and let's do this. Your one simple decision has already started the ripple of change—nice work! You have now become an integral part of this tribe that is changing the world. From the depths of my soul I thank you for stepping up. Your future self, tribe, and every woman who didn't get to have the opportunity to use her voice or follow her dreams is relying on you to follow your bliss.

Your sister in bliss,
Lori Harder

HOW TO BEGIN INVITING YOUR TRIBE

Turn the page for the invitation that you can use to help build your tribe. It is your way to ask others if they want to share this experience with you. You can either purchase two or three other copies to start your tribe now or send them the following link with the invite to join your tribe and opportunity to purchase their own: atribecalledbliss.com. And just like in life, after you complete one step, the rest will be revealed. You don't have to see the entire staircase as long as you trust I will always give you the next step—and for that you have my word. Just take the first step and the process will magically unravel.

WITH THIS BOOK
I WOULD LIKE TO EXTEND
A SACRED INVITATION TO JOIN

A TRIBE CALLED BLISS

Dear _____:

I gift you this book and extend an invite to our new Bliss Tribe, because you are a woman I admire and whom I would like to connect with on a deeper level. Bound by the agreements and inspired by the lessons and pursuits inside this book, I believe we can have a beautiful connection that doesn't take away from our time and energy, but instead restores, recharges, and adds more value to our lives.

A Bliss Tribe is a group of women who know with certainty that there is more to be experienced in this lifetime than what is seen on the surface. We sense our calling to crack surface layers and live in a more meaningful way. We are done suppressing, shrinking, and shying away from our light. We learn to accept uncertainty and failure and get excited to bloom from under the dirt in which we were buried. We no longer choose to travel alone and have a mutual interest in elevating ourselves as much as we do each other. We believe that when we come from a place of service and adding value to another woman's life, we will be abundantly blessed and taken care of. We agree to act, speak, and show up in accordance with the highest good in order to fulfill our potential and follow our bliss. We forgive ourselves quickly and share our fears to eradicate the power of the stories that are stopping us. We refuse to settle for a life unlived. We are sisters in the arena together and we go further faster while having way more fun.

Tribes thrive on structure and agreements, which will be clearly laid out in this book for us to follow. A Bliss Tribe has a "Tribe Meeting" and "Tribe Discussions" guided by this book for one hour, every other week. Our tribe agrees to never go over time, respect all the rules, and always honor our consistent appointment. If this is not the right time, or you don't feel called to this commitment or connection, please know this book is still a gift for you to read on your own or to build your own tribe.

If you feel called to a radical new way of living and to stepping into your highest potential, please RSVP by emailing _____ with a "YES I'm ready to connect to my tribe!"

HOW THIS BOOK WORKS

YOU KNOW THOSE PARTS OF BOOKS YOU THINK YOU CAN SKIP? THIS IS NOT ONE. PLEASE MAKE SURE YOU READ THIS . . .

Before I write another word, I know this book implies that I want you to use it to form a tribe and read through it together. That is because my intention is to give you the structure and gift of a tribe based on the agreements and self-work that has led me to my bliss. But if you just don't quite feel ready for that yet, you can still go through this book and do the Soul Assignments on your own. I know that after you read this book once, you will feel curious enough to then forge forward toward expanding your perception of what you are capable of doing, receiving, and, most importantly, giving.

This is not your mama's self-help book, her book club, or a modern woman's guide to networking. This certainly isn't trying to teach you the old-school business mastermind format. It's a collaboration with your soul and your future chosen sisters, enriching each other's experience and learning to accept yourself while traveling through this masterpiece called life—and my sweet baby flame, when we practice this, together, you ignite possibility and bliss.

This book is broken into three sections for you to get the most out of it personally and as a tribe. The three sections were created specifically because these are the hidden places where we stop ourselves without realizing it. This book and all the lessons in it will finally give you the exact tools, insights, and scripts to transcend those blockades that always send you back to square one in your relationships and your goals.

Section 1 is about the New Way of Building Your Community. It's your foundation for the whole book. In this section I share my personal story about why I am so passionate about tribe and how it has catapulted my life. Together we will look at what has been stopping you from having the kind of tribe you desire in your life, why tribe is so dang vital, and then we will get SUPER specific on how to build your own. Once you feel fully equipped, which you will by the end of the section, you will actually create a real-life tribe of your own with which to go throughout the rest of this book.

Section 2 is the New Way of Being. This section begins your regular set tribal meetings to review each chapter together and do the Tribe Work after each one. When I reference the New Way of Being, I mean the new way of how you will show up for yourself, to the world and in your relationships. It's a set of ideas and guiding principles of how to be in your daily life, think and interact as your highest, most authentic self. It's like a girl code that will keep your mindset and tribe from falling prey to what may have taken them down in the past.

Section 3 is all about the New Way of Belonging. When I

say "belonging" in the book, it does not mean trying to fit in. It does not mean changing who you are. It means becoming more of who you are and having the willingness to show the world the real you. Belonging takes courage, forgiveness, and acceptance of our past, uncovering and taking complete ownership of our own magic. Belonging means being comfortable with your brilliance *and* darkness until you find those excited to share in your journey for who you are. In this section you'll read lessons and do exercises with your tribe to gain tools to uncover and reclaim yourself and your right of belonging to yourself. When you are clear about who you are and have the tools to connect to yourself, you don't worry about belonging, because you will know that you do.

I promise if you use this book the way it is intended, your life is about to get better than you could have ever imagined, and your new tribe connections are not only going to feel like long-lost sisters, but you will begin showing up for yourself in a way you never imagined. This book holds the map to uncover the real you in order to manifest the relationships you've been missing because of who you're not yet being. That's all about to change, and while it will take work, it's also going to be more fun and fulfilling than just about anything else you've ever experienced. That's a big statement because everything in these pages that I ask you to "try on" is the work I do that makes me obsessed with my life and the people in it.

section one

THE NEW WAY OF BUILDING YOUR COMMUNITY

Like I said earlier, this section provides everything you need to know about how and why your own bliss requires you to build your new community, or as we will start referring to it in this book, your new Bliss Tribe. Before we take off, though, I feel it's vital I share this very important preflight announcement—otherwise known as my story from small-town girl with panic attacks, anxiety, body-weight and image struggles, little education, zero confidence, few friends, and a strict religious upbringing, to a blissed-out successful entrepreneur, speaker, fitness model, confident, tribe-building motha! So fancy, right? Those accomplishments listed above are nice—not gonna pretend they aren't. I want those things for you, too, but I also like to know all of you, including the mess behind all the stuff because *that* is the real *STUFF*. I love the dirt, the thorns, and the rain, because without all of it, there are no roses and certainly no bliss. But before we go on this journey together, I think you and I need to make our own personal connection so that you can know where I'm coming from and that *I really do see you*. It's important I share the significant events that brought me to my ~~knees~~ bliss. Stand by as I reveal my whole soul to you . . . My armpits are sweating already—here goes. My only ask is that if I show you mine, you show me yours.

one

BORN FOR BLISS

The summers were hot and the days were long. There was dirt under my fingernails, scabs on my knees, and the baby hairs around my face were as wild as I was. I was eight years old, and my only job was to keep an eye out for all adventures and anything that needed exploring in my neighborhood. Each day ended with an all-out adrenaline rush. As evening gave way to night I raced my bike back to headquarters, flying through yards and streets without sidewalks, to get home in time to avoid any trouble with the bosses.

I knew my terrain. I knew where the roots of the trees had cracked the pavement in just the right place to create the oh-so-perfect jump. Pedal like a madwoman, and you'd catch some serious air. I could show you the secret shortcut—through three of my neighbors' yards, past a creepy old barn, and down a tiny pathway between two old abandoned garages that only a kid could fit through—that led straight to a candy-filled convenience store where you could turn in pop cans for spare change and leave adorned in layers of candy necklaces and fingers full of Ring Pops.

Back then, "weird" was my calling card. I loved that I was everyone's first exposure to the unparalleled sensory experience of licking roll-on deodorant. Just watch your tongue go from damp to shockingly dry in under a second. Baby powder cigarette, anyone? It's pretty incredible what you can do with a drinking straw, a square of toilet paper, a dash of baby powder, and a mini rubber band—and a lot of idle time. My mom always wondered why the entire bathroom was coated with a light dusting of white, but I couldn't bring myself to tell her I just couldn't quit Johnson & Johnson. I had so many tricks and talents—why hide them from the world? I wrote fake personal ads, pecking away on our old typewriter, giggling to myself the whole time picturing how hard my mom and sister would laugh when they read them. I created watercolor masterpieces, selling my work in my front yard for a dollar. People—mostly my family—*okay, just my family*—would buy my shitty drawings, but sales nonetheless! My favorite past times included baking cookies with my mom, singing with my dad, and making leaf crowns with my sister. I forced my family to listen to my karaoke songs and watch my choreographed dance routines night after night after dinner. I was becoming a true performer and this called for the right outfit, which meant asking my mom to buy me the perfect ballerina dress from the JCPenney catalogue. A full tutu made of fluffy white tulle with a shimmery, ivory bodice, making me feel like a swan when I moved (because obviously in my mind I moved with the exact same grace as the glorious white bird). I wore that thing until it pulled my shoulders forward and my bum had no choice but to eat the spandex. I looked like the hunchback of Notre Dame headed to her first prom.

Life was good. My biggest stress was blue jeans that wouldn't "tight roll" and tube socks that wouldn't stay up—"quitters." My fears were the campfire stories that told of a man with a hook for a hand, the monsters lurking under my bed, or the gremlins I was convinced would come out of my toilet at night. Never pee with the lights out—that's when they get you.

It was a completely magical and mysterious time, being an eight-year-old in the woods of Upper Michigan (The U.P.). I was living in the era of freedom, in the age of bliss. I cruised around my neighborhood on my Banana Seat Hog feeling like the mayor, handlebar streamers on point, with my boom box playing Debbie Gibson in my basket.

I loved that girl. I had no idea how quickly I would lose HER.

TRADING BLISS

The invite came Sunday after church, from a close friend. Her family was gathering a group of kids to go swimming, and asked if I would I like to come? *Yes!* Because this wasn't just your ordinary swim gathering, it was THE swim gathering with all of the kids that I had grown up with—I was eleven years old. It was an evening swim at our recreation center and they had an impressive Olympic-size pool complete with three tiers of diving boards. They picked me up in their minivan. We crammed in, all of us making bets on who would jump off the platform and who wouldn't. I loved swimming. I loved zipping my legs up and flipping my fin like a mermaid, or dragging my hair back and forth in slow fluid strokes watching it as if it was silk. I felt so free in the water, where my body always felt light and graceful. In the water, you could be whatever you wanted to be and try anything you wanted to try, because water is consistent, reliable, and always there to give you a soft, safe place to land.

Eventually, my turn to jump came. I stood at the base of the ladder that led to the diving board, so excited to show off yet another brilliant skill of mine. Would I dive, do a flip, or spread eagle? So many choices to impress the crowd. As I started my ascent, I could see him, floating along the side of the pool, flanked by my two friends, girls who were pretty, skinny, and shaped nothing like me. I knew that my crush had his eyes on these girls, but I believed in time he would change his gaze. As I was about to jump, I heard the cheering begin. I listened closer, thinking they were daring me with a trick they wanted to see me try. Little did they know I could handle whatever they threw at me!

"Whale . . . whale . . . whale . . ." The words became crystal clear. "Whale . . . whale . . . whale . . ." I saw his mouth say the words. I heard the words. I was blindsided. "Don't jump in the pool, you whale!" the kids yelled. "There won't be any water left for us!"

There I was, at the top, looking down at the crowd—completely stunned. I felt naked, embarrassed, ashamed. I couldn't breathe. All I could do to survive was jump. No flip, no dive, no tricks— just get me underwater so I can hide. The water enveloped and folded around me as I let out my heartbreak and pain through a screaming sob under the surface of the pool. Bubbles flew past my face. I was sinking. I let it take me under. I could not picture coming up. *I hate them. I hate me. I am disgusting.* My heartbreak was so intense that the moment of pain became tattooed on my soul, and the shame of who I was physically set in. How could I love something I was ashamed of?

The trade was done. And just like that, SHE was gone.

INHERITED TRIBE

I was never obese but I was also never thin. I come from a long line of women (and men) who struggle with their weight. "Bad genetics," I have been told by my family over and over again. "You will struggle your whole life," I would hear my family say. "It's the Baker way! Just wait, you'll be fat like the rest of us." My mom was a Baker, and this idea of having to go to battle with my body is what I would carry with me through my preteen years and into my adult life. Never did I think to examine our habits or beliefs, because everyone around me did the same thing, and it was confirmed that *Fat* was our family's curse.

I was just "lil tubs," but my big sister was "BIG tubs." The torment for her started early, in elementary school. She lived a life of incessant dieting and early-morning workouts, sweating it out with aerobics tapes well before the rest of us were even out of bed. But it didn't take long before I was following in her exact footsteps. We grew up watching the women in our family diet. This is just what we did. Some families went on trips. We went on diets.

Sure, weight was an easy target for all of the bullying that BIG tubs and lil tubs endured at school, but it wasn't the only material the kids had to work with to create their torment. In Upper Michigan where there is zero diversity, being different stands out like a sore thumb. Being raised in a restrictive religion where we didn't celebrate holidays, birthdays, or say the Pledge of Allegiance meant leaving the classroom during all holiday art projects, school plays, and celebrations. We had to sit down while everyone was standing with their hand on their heart every morning and pass on all the birthday songs and goodies. Not only did we have to say "No, thank you" to the Tupperware container of mouth-watering birthday cupcakes, we were counseled against associating with anyone outside of our religion—ever. For my sister and me, dating was strictly off-limits until you were old enough to be married, and when that time came, all dates until marriage would still require a chaperone and this made for plenty of comments about my sexuality. Needless to say, knocking on my classmates' doors, or interrupting their slumber parties and Saturday morning cartoons to ask if they wanted to hear about the Bible, did not help my reputation. Yup, that happened.

Although I participated in the religious activities expected of me, I always carried the burden of "never being good enough" or "being able to do enough to be saved." I lived every day in complete and utter fear that the world would end any minute, and I would end with it. Every time my peers would threaten to chase me off their porch with a shotgun, call me a weirdo or a lesbian, I felt my guts tearing open. I wanted so desperately to do good, to feel safe, to be saved, and to know I was loved.

WE BECOME OUR TRIBE

In time I learned to do my own thing. I hung out with my family and tagged along with my older sister's friends. One of my fa-

vorite things to do was to go to the grocery store with my mom.
I could always score the food I wanted and talk her into buying
some fitness magazines for me. With our cart looking like we
were preparing for the end of the world, we'd head to the check-
out counter, unload everything on the belt, and make small talk
with the cashier.

"Pay and meet me outside," she'd said in a panic on one of
our many grocery runs. "You are going to have to drive home." It
was half-shock and half-thrill. I was thirteen and thankfully had
been driving with my parents many times before this. This was
the first I could remember seeing her have a severe panic attack
that she appeared to have no control over.

Anxiety would soon take over my mother, and I'm pretty sure
her mother had suffered from it too. It intensified as I grew older,
or perhaps with the major financial struggles of my parents' going
bankrupt and losing their business or the surprise that was my
little brother in the midst of all of it. I hated seeing how she felt,
so I would do anything I could to help her out around the house.
My room was spotless. I did my chores and then some. I learned
how to make those perfect vacuum lines in the carpet, which became an obsession. In my quest for perfection, I never shared my
struggles, my fears, or my secrets. I would do anything I could to
avoid being a burden and not add any unnecessary stress.

One day at school not long after watching and hearing my
mother talk about her panic attacks, I had *my* first attack. I was
reading out loud to my class—one of my very favorite things to do.
I could captivate my audience by giving the characters different
voices and funny accents, and it was the one thing that awarded
me compliments from my fellow students and recognition from

my teachers. But this particular day something changed. "Aren't you nervous?" my brain asked me out of the blue. "You have anxiety." A few words into the first paragraph, and I couldn't read. I felt dizzy. Tears flooded my eyes and I couldn't hear my words over my heartbeat pounding in my ears. I thought I was dying.

"I can't read anymore," I told the teacher. I excused myself to the bathroom, where I let the crazy play itself out. This would be the last time I would voluntarily raise my hand for a very long time. From that day on, the panic attacks increased and I'd experience anxiety any time the attention was focused solely on me. My fun-loving days as a performer were over. My inner conflict began and my identity changed.

I convinced my parents to homeschool me through high school.

Running away from the problem was the perfect way to cope with my anxiety, and the way to stop the bullying. I would never be like the other kids anyway. My parents told me homeschooling was not a good idea for me. They would not have the time or be able to teach me what I needed, but I pleaded. I gathered so much evidence from the other kids in my church who were homeschooled and made such a giant case around my anxiety attacks that my parents had no choice. At the time it was a popular thing to do in our church, a way for us kids to not be exposed to all of the "inappropriate" behavior that happens during high school years. I used my sister's nightmarish stories of bullying, temptation, underage partying, and boys to show them how they would be keeping me safe. *Pretty good, huh?*

"I have panic attacks, and I struggle with my weight." This

was my story, and I played it over and over again. My family understood it—they had the same story, and somehow the pain made us closer at times. Still, I yearned for a better way to manage this. I refused to swallow that I would have to feel this way the rest of my life.

After joining my sister in some workouts, I noticed that my anxiety was more manageable when I would exercise. Over time I noticed I thought clearer, slept better, and wouldn't feel as anxious on days that I worked out. This desire to want to stop feeling like my life was spiraling out of control fueled my love affair with fitness. Most days I hated exercising, but I knew how much better I would feel afterward. It was food that remained my biggest challenge.

The eating habits of my family continued their yo-yo cycle of dieting and bingeing, dieting, bingeing . . . I might exercise my butt off, but I was no different. If I was on a diet, I was all in—Malt-O-Meal breakfast, diet pop, Lean Cuisine for lunch, and chicken with plain white rice for dinner. If I wasn't on a diet, I ate like it was my last meal—two heaping platefuls of spaghetti covered in parmesan cheese, dinner rolls with butter, and a giant bowl of ice cream covered in Marshmallow Fluff and hot fudge.

Working out and staying busy made me feel much more balanced, which helped me manage the ups and downs of emotions that came from being sedentary and relying on food. I started to see myself in more of an athletic light, which lessened my self-loathing a bit, but this ongoing mental struggle with food made me feel like a prisoner. Because working out was one of the only things in my life I felt I could control, my obsession was solidified, especially since I would immediately put on weight from my eating habits if I wasn't doing it.

I was still carrying this belief, this fear of food and what was coming for me. I never knew if the next corner I would turn would hold my fate of getting fat or having another panic episode. Somehow in my soul I knew that as soon as I was old enough, I would have to remove myself as much as possible from the people that were reinforcing my fears until I was strong enough to stand firm in my new ideas—even in the face of adversity. This would be the only way to move past this.

A DIFFERENT TRIBE

I met Bree when I was fourteen. She was beautiful, outgoing, fit, and fearless. She was in the same religion as I was, yet I had never known anyone like her. She walked into the room like she was ten feet tall, so proud of who she was, and when she left the energy left with her. She was such an alien of impossibility. Of course I felt instantly drawn to her. Her family was visiting our congregation from another town. We were both so excited to meet someone our own age who had similar interests that we decided to be pen pals. It wasn't long before I was convincing my parents to let her parents pick me up at the "halfway point" so we could spend weeks at a time at each other's house to make the drive worth it. We lived a few hours apart and this became a normal thing until one of us started driving. Before then, our long-distance phone bills were a constant battle in both of our homes.

"When do we eat our snacks?" I asked the first night I stayed at her house. We had just ended a really active day outside, all day swimming, hiking, and getting lost around town. "What do you mean?" she asked. "We just had dinner! We don't really have snacks, but we have apples." My brain went into overdrive. *An apple?! For real? I'm bordering on sugar withdrawal, and this chick wants to give me an apple? For the love of all things holy, Bree, please tell me you at least have some damn peanut butter or caramel sauce for it!* "Sure, I'll take an apple."

The first time I spent a week at Bree's house I not only was flabbergasted by how different her family was than mine, but I also lost five pounds. There was a totally different way of being, thinking, eating, and living. I just assumed every family of my faith was the same, but this week proved to me that there was an entirely different way to live. The week unfolded and so did the realization that they didn't snack—WTF? What do they do all night? In fact, they ate three fairly hearty meals a day—and that was pretty much it. Bree's family didn't seem to have an emotional tie to food, and their lifestyle made it blaringly clear that my family did. Food just wasn't a big deal or topic of conversation or something you bonded over like it was in my family. They didn't have a goodie drawer, a cracker-laden cabinet, or even a hidden bag of chocolate chips. You would simply eat dinner and drink some water or milk before bed. I wasn't actually starving, but my brain had so much trouble breaking this habit of snacking that I struggled all week looking for traces of candy, chips, crackers—anything!

On top of this, they were very laid-back. They had a thriving business, took trips, and seemed proud of the fact that they made decent money. They expected their kids to get some extra education, where in my particular congregation, college seemed discouraged. Each visit to Bree's was shifting my paradigm, shattering the ways I thought things had to be. There was definitely never any talk of fears, anxiety, or panic attacks. Everyone was so outgoing, bold, and confident that they must have thought you were weird if you weren't that way. At their house, I became an entirely different version of myself. It was so fun letting this version come out that I would dread going home because in my mind I turned home into the place where I fell into the habits that make me feel bad. I didn't want to get fat, I didn't want to be anxious, and I didn't want to live in fear. I wanted to be a part of her tribe, which was so different, so accepting, so fun, so me, and so free.

The years passed and Bree and I became pretty inseparable, along with two other girls, Melissa and Stella. Bree's house became the hub, where we would all drive to to meet. I was learning more and more that these "rules" were not hard and fast, but were dependent upon who was running the "tribe," or in my case, the congregation.

The more I experienced outside of my normal life, the more I closed off to my family. It's not that I didn't want my parents to know me, or to be close with my sister, but I felt I was protecting them from having to make a choice between the religion and me—my ideas and theirs. My friends and I were not abiding by the agreements of our church. We were no longer the kids we were all expected to be. We had broken agreements right and left, and if anyone found out, we would have to answer for our actions and most likely be excommunicated like the other kids we knew that got caught drinking, unchaperoned underage dating, going to concerts, or dabbling in drugs. Our hunger for self-expression and freedom kept us all in agreement to have each other's backs.

LEAVING THE TRIBE

I chose to live a separate, hidden life. I spent my teenage years in suppression, fear, and extreme guilt over what I now know is totally normal teenage behavior. At home, I still respected my parents, did my chores, and followed the rules. In fact, I was a really hard-working kid. I showed up three days a week in church and also went door to door to preach a couple times a week. But I hated that I was lying to my family; however, had I told them who I had become they would have had no choice but to tell the congregation—because not sharing a wrongdoing was as if you were doing it, too. It was their job to do this due diligence to help save the person. The penalty could mean excommunication, and I just couldn't take the risk of the pain of being cast out from all I ever knew. Most of all I could not hurt my family that deeply or live in that type of isolation. I felt like a caged wild animal. It didn't matter how loving my parents were, and they were. I could not be *me*, listen to what I wanted, wear what I liked, or express my actual thoughts on religion and relationships, or share the fact that I had big dreams and did NOT want to live a life of financial struggle and mental guilt. I wanted to run far away, where no one could judge me, keep their eyes on me, or tell me I was not worthy of love because of the things I had done. This "double life" was eating me alive. Did God really want me to feel all of this shame, guilt, and fear every day?

The only brief relief from shame and fear I felt was when I

was exercising or getting drunk with my friends, and I counted the days to freedom. I knew exactly where I was moving to when I turned eighteen—to Madison, Wisconsin. I knew some people there who were going to college, including Bree, and I was going to work full-time.

I broke my mom's heart when I left. She couldn't understand why I wanted to leave so soon and I couldn't stand to think about the disappointment if I told her. I drove my tiny Geo Metro that I paid $500 cash for up to my new apartment. My parents drove separately to help get me settled in. All we could afford was a one-bedroom apartment, which we filled with two blow-up chairs that would constantly lose all their air, a TV with no cable connection, and an answering machine. I was working three different waitressing jobs at once—one in the afternoon, one in the evening, and one a few late nights a week cocktail waitressing. I knew five different ways to sing "Happy Birthday" with their accompanied dances and wore horrible clownish costumes at the two themed chain restaurants. The first was TGI Fridays, where I had to suit up in a ridiculous hat, suspenders with hundreds of pins, and a referee shirt. The second admittedly was Hooters, which meant wearing dance tights, tube socks, white high tops, and wretched orange shorts that looked terrible on everyone. The third was a dive bar that served food from metal buckets late at night. I would cry in my car en route from one crap hole to the next. I started smoking at work because smoke breaks were when the only human connection happened—along with anything that resembled a break. I was working more than I ever thought possible, barely paying my bills, hardly sleeping, and going out with friends seven days a week. I lived in three states—depressed, hungover, or drunk. My tiny amount of normalcy was when I made it to the gym a few times a week.

My friends were living the same life as me, the only difference being the addition of college classes. I knew I had a drinking problem, but some of their habits made me feel better about my choices. One friend would take a beer into the shower with her each morning, jokingly telling me she was "off to the beach," which made me feel like I was the one "winning at life" by comparison.

At one point Bree and I decided we needed a real vacation, so we got together some friends and planned a trip. Cancún, a week that began and ended at the pool bar. Sunburns, margaritas, and guacamole. Toward the end of the week we met some guys from the Midwest at our hotel. We'd been drinking all day and decided to go dancing with them that night. Bree was drunk when we arrived at the club, so I left her sleeping in a booth with Melissa and some other friends as her babysitters. I needed to find a bathroom in this sea of sweaty bodies and flailing limbs. Once I came back, most everyone was gone. "Where did everyone go?" I asked the few stragglers who were still at the table we were at. "One of the guys took Bree back to the hotel," they said, and they didn't know where Melissa and the others went.

I panicked thinking about Bree and how I didn't really trust the guys we came with, and I was also worried about Melissa. My heart pounded; I ran out of the club onto the busy street. The bus would take forever so I hailed a cab, jumped in the front seat, and gave the driver the name of our hotel. It was past midnight and the city was alive, pumping the driver with salsa music, lights, and crowds everywhere. The cab driver started small-talking in broken English and asked if I liked Biggie Smalls, but all I could think about was if Bree was okay. He popped a cassette tape into the dash, and "Big Poppa" started playing.

"I don't think we're going the right way," I finally said, feeling a bit of worry for myself. The lights of the city were gone and "Big Poppa" was on its third replay. He told me that we were taking a shortcut to my hotel, which calmed me a bit, because I'd get to Bree faster. Eventually, there were no more lights, the road had narrowed, and the jungle had grown thick around us. "Where are we?" Another back way, I learned, as he turned down a hidden road, reassuring me that it was okay and that he just "had to use the bathroom." *No, no, no, no, this isn't right,* a voice inside my head screamed. A few hundred feet, and the car was swaddled by tall grass, palms, vines, and trees. He opened the door to find a place to go to the bathroom. I could no longer see him and my senses fired on all cylinders, the awareness of each bead of sweat on my skin, my heartbeat like a bass drum, eyes wide, and breathing shallow. I took off my platform heels and wrapped the straps around each of my hands. *I will fight,* the voice said.

He came through my passenger door, throwing his muscular, enraged body on top of mine, wrapping his hands around my neck. I couldn't access air, and the blood that filled my ears made it hard to hear him yelling. He wanted money, and something else I couldn't understand, but all I could do was claw at his face—just to get air. Just as my vision started going black, he let go. I told him that all I had was money for cab fare, but this made him angry. He started punching me repeatedly in the face and I fought back, beating him with my shoes.

We fought for what seemed like forever—a cycle of strangulation, near passing out, letting go, again and again. Until I wrestled him off of me, slid into the driver's seat, and shoved him out the passenger side with my legs. I threw the car in reverse, hands shaking and tasting my freedom. *SMASH* . . . I hit a rock. The car stopped. This felt like the end and my heart sank. He was back inside and I felt something sharp on the skin of my neck. I started screaming, but that only made him push the utility knife deeper. He forced me to strip down to my underwear; he was threatening to kill me.

I struggled in the cab for hours that night. Threats, beatings, punches, a knife held to my throat, and sexual assault.

Suddenly I realized that he didn't want to kill me, because he easily could have. *It will all be okay*, I heard a clear voice in my head say. I felt a sort of calm come over me. *You will be okay.* Words starting falling out of my mouth that didn't feel like my own. Out of the blue I began to tell him about my family. I told him about my faith in God. I told him that if he let me go, then all of this would be okay. He would be forgiven and it would be forgotten. Because God knows his heart.

I watched the monster soften. I saw glimpses of a human being, a man.

He told me that this was the first time he had done something like this, that he needs money. "It's okay . . . it was just a mistake," I said. "Once you drop me off, you will have a chance to start again."

He took me back, but only on the condition that my head be in his lap with the knife to my throat. I complied. He dropped me off a block away from my hotel, making me promise not to look back. I didn't.

The sun was just beginning to break the darkness. I walked slowly for a few steps, then sprinted straight to the hotel. I had two black eyes and was bleeding from my neck. My teeth were chipped and my face swollen and bruised. Shoes in hand, clothes ripped and spotted with blood, I walked into the lobby. The people at the front desk rushed to my assistance. The reality of what just took place started to hit me. I started to shake as I asked them to call the police for me. The adrenaline had subsided and the physical pain was starting to set in.

I spent the next day at the hospital, and then with the police. I still wasn't sure what had just happened, if it was me or something else choosing my words. I just knew that I was not alone and all the right things came out of my mouth during the attack. The voice had been guiding my every move, and I felt grateful to be alive. A female officer told me that this sort of occurrence happens more often than you would think, and that I was lucky to be alive and in as good of shape as I was. I was sent home with a souvenir—a shoddy police report, written on a typewriter that had about five keys missing. As soon as I left, so did any attempt at finding him.

When I arrived home, I desperately needed to process what had happened. I was dealing with a slew of emotions that were bubbling forth from the trauma, and I was scared to be alone, scared of men, and angry at the world. I started to share details with Bree. "You can't talk about this," she said. "I can't hear about it. It makes me sick to my stomach." She told me to not talk about it, and that would make it go away. This was the advice she lived by, so I figured it would work for me too. So I stopped talking about it. I did not want to be a burden to the people closest to me. I knew it upset people, and I felt ashamed that I was drunk, that I wore a short dress, and that I was irresponsible enough to have let it all happen. I felt responsible for what I had brought into my life. I never told my family, and I didn't talk about it again until years later.

I became hardened. Combative. I lived on edge. The world was no longer a safe place for me, and I had to adopt a new way of living. *Never think. Never feel.* This was my new motto, the motto of my friends. Thinking is bad. Feeling is worse. Stay busy. Stay numb. More parties. More alcohol.

THERE'S GOT TO BE MORE . . .

The highs of this way of life were becoming less high, and the lows felt like they were getting lower. And there was a voice in my head that started getting louder. *SHE* seemed to be screaming "This is not who you are!" One thing was becoming crystal clear, this tribe I was hanging around was going down fast, and I was going down with them, and this voice wasn't going to let me sleepwalk through life without paying for it. She was ruining the temporary fix of parties, people, booze, shopping, and men. She would not be quieted, and she did not approve of my choices. And she wasn't just making my days unbearable—she started waking me up from my sleep in the middle of the night. I was in terrible pain. It felt like it had taken on a physical form. I was hurting people I loved, and even worse, I was hurting and suffocating my soul. I wanted to leave my body, abort my brain, run from my life. I couldn't stand to be alone with myself. I couldn't escape. I hated what I was tolerating and who I had become. I felt anxious, stressed, and like a complete loser—all the time.

A few more years passed before I started to "get it." The nudges had turned into two-by-fours to the face, because clearly the "hard way" was the only way I would ever learn. I wasn't clear on what I should do, but I was clear on what I couldn't do anymore. I gathered as much of a plan as I could before I quit my job. I severed toxic relationships. I moved states. I started over with nothing but some credit card debt to my name. I did the last thing I ever wanted to do in the world, and that was move back in with my parents with my tail between my legs. I slept in my younger brother's old bedroom, in a bed with dinosaurs and *Star Wars* figurines decorating the headboard, and glow-in-the-dark stars on the ceiling. I spent the next year trying to pick up the pieces from the last three years I had spent being the raging bull in the china shop—that was my life. I'll share more later . . . I had to figure out who I was. What in the world was this pain and the screaming from my soul trying to tell me? I was spending all of my time working to pay off bills and working out at the gym to stay sane. I was lonely and lost, and my heart ached.

It was time to send in the search-and-rescue team. I had to find my bliss.

two

BUT FIRST, BLISS

Every day, everywhere in the world, in every language, people ask each other the question: "How are you?" and, under most everyone's automated answer of "I'm fine," you will find layers of inner turmoil, insecurity, and struggle. It's as though we are all waiting for someone to anoint us to be better than fine, to finally feel desirable, promotable, worthy, or ready for this highly sought-after utopian place we call bliss. If I've learned one thing in my years of bliss chasing, it's this: you can upgrade to glossy surroundings, get special titles and degrees, and put yourself in a world among fancy things and fancy people, but you will not find bliss. No matter how much hope and validation you put on someone's approval or a destination—those are not bliss. If bliss means getting things, permission, validation, or reaching a destination, you'll miss a lifetime full of it.

Bliss. The very word conjured up a superlative land filled with white sand beaches, eternal sunsets, a magazine-cover body, millions of social media followers, a fulfilling career, boundless energy, intoxicatingly passionate romcom–worthy love, a closet full of designer clothes inside of my designer home, Girl Boss money, a never-ending agenda of fun, friends, fulfillment, and champagne.

More baffling yet, when we are asked to define what bliss is we tend to just name more things or achievements that we don't yet have "enough" of. But why does bliss never seem to translate into everyday life? Perhaps it's the lack of a clear definition, or maybe it doesn't seem within reach, or maybe, like I thought, it's a place where you have all the things that finally make you lovable by all. We're constantly chasing after objects (or people) we desire in order to reach bliss. There is yet another problem with bliss—even if you've experienced a glimpse of what it could be in your life, you can't stop it from disappearing. Trying to hold on to bliss can feel like trying to turn a wild bird into your shoulder pet.

Is bliss really that elusive? What is it? Let's start talking about defining what bliss is not. Brace yourself—it is not a place we travel to. It is not an object we desire. It is not another human being. Bliss has no physical form. Bliss is not: a man, a title, a woman, a baby, a job, a soul mate, a promotion, a trophy, a house, a proud set of parents, a smokin' hot body, someone's apology, someone's adoration, a higher degree, a big bank account, a closet full of clothes and shoes, or even paradise. I know this, because I have had—or should I say forced, tackled, and kung-fu gripped—most of the above. I have been chasing bliss all the way from my childhood in Upper Michigan where I literally tackled boys on the playground in grade school and forced them to kiss me (they were not happy about it and neither were their mothers) to the long winters living in the Midwest to my last five years in sunny Southern California, from struggling with my weight to being on fitness magazine covers, from having a negative bank account to having millions of dollars. It's taken me some time, but I've been on both sides of the fence—from nothing—to everything I've ever wanted—to losing it all—to getting it all back and being afraid of losing it all again—to being okay with that entire crazy cycle. I've now got a pretty good idea of what bliss actually is.

Not many people are walking around feeling blissful, or even remotely happy, for that matter. Despite living in one of the most desirable places on earth (sunny California), I see this everywhere I go, and when I ask people, "What's blocking you from feeling truly happy?" I get a variety of very valid (and not-so-valid) responses, ranging from traumatic childhood memories to stories of financial struggle, being ghosted by a lover, politics, traffic, or a bad cup of coffee that morning. I myself used to tote around a laundry list of things I blamed as to why I was Not Able To Be Happy: I was raised in a very prohibitive religion and the particular congregation I was in had me living in constant fear and I believed my sins would not be forgiven and I was not good enough to be saved at Armageddon, aka the end of the world, which I believed was right around the corner; my family had money struggles; inherited anxiety and poor genetics; traumatic experiences in my teen years; kidnapping in Mexico; sexual assault; stolen car; lost jobs; cheating boyfriends; cheating on boyfriends . . . on and on and on, into my late twenties these experiences defined me and I clung to them for reasons why "I can't." My list could wind its way around a few city blocks—but

I'll spare you. Eventually, I put down my list, which made some room for bliss to enter my life—but not before creating pure pandemonium.

Throughout this book, I am going to share with you how I define bliss, where I searched, and finally how I found bliss. You will learn the most effective ways to spend your time and energy—and the most ineffective. Together we will create the foundation for your tribe to get to the bottom of what bliss means to you, how you attain it, and even how you sustain it without killing yourself (or wasting time like I did).

Bliss, much like all the other feelings we are blessed to experience for different reference points of bliss, is your innate gift. While bliss doesn't deny the fact that "life happens," it does give you the ability to reframe and see everything in a way that supports you and allows you to return quickly to a place of peace and love. No matter how you define it, bliss is different for all of us, and I am not here to define it for you—I can only explain my experience of how I live in bliss more often than not, in hopes to be a guide for yours.

Bliss for me boils down to giving gratitude and purpose, or as I see it, everything that comes with the following of one's bliss. It's in the things big and small, the highs and lows, in the simple and the complex, through the struggles and the successes. Bliss is my morning gratitude and prayer, the smell that only happens early in the day after a cool moonlit night, the warmth of my coffee mug in my hands while I savor the last quiet moments of the morning, the feeling of a shower so hypnotizing you want to enjoy five more minutes. Bliss is the pain of something ending and leaving space for renewal. Bliss is in the tasks I get to do throughout the day that I used to wish I was needed for. Bliss is the gap between my goals that I used to wish I could skip over. Bliss is knowing I have the power over my feelings and not giving it away to someone else. Bliss is trusting myself. My bliss is feeling fully expressed, unapologetically me, and feeling an unshakable sense of acceptance, alignment, and belonging within my own self.

Let me give another illustration of bliss—I ran into a friend and we shared a quick hug. Her perfume was so unique, yet instantly detectable from a past memory. It was like those moments when a single whiff of something sends you time traveling and suddenly you're back there in full color . . . I was transported to age eight or nine, playing outside near my old-lady neighbor's prized rose bushes we were never allowed to pick but always snuck a bud or two. I snapped back to the present and I asked her what it was. "It's an entire rose bush made into botanicals." She went on to tell me the healing properties of the entire rose and how she loves it because it's not just about the pretty petals, but it's everything that supports the beauty—the stem, the leaves, the roots and thorns. "It's not just the rose itself, but it's the parts we look over and normally want to throw out or get rid of that have a purpose. It's ALL of it."

Bliss, much like success, is B.Y.O.D.—By Your Own Definition. I will give you the tools to reveal it, but ultimately you will have to decide exactly what it is for you so you can work to feel it and take notice when you are in it. The most astonishing part of it all is that your life doesn't have to change in big or dramatic ways to reach bliss, but it will be tiny shifts internally that begin to dramatically change what you physically see in your world. But I'm warning you, you may shift so much that your current life seems like a completely new one.

Now, I want you to scan your mind and body for the smallest, tiniest part of you that wants to trust that you can experience this bliss feeling someday. That little tiny nudge, that little freckle of faith is all you need to begin a bliss tsunami.

three

WHY TRIBE?

Walking with a friend in the dark is better than walking alone in the light.

—HELEN KELLER

"How did you get where you are?" I get asked that question—a lot. "I worked hard and got A LOT of help." That is my short and, to some, not-so-desirable answer. But it's the truth—I would not have gotten here—to this blissful place of loving my career, my people, my life, and myself—without a lot of help from other people and a lot of work. The reason why my answer is great news for you is because it means I didn't get here by having some sort of special talent or ability that you don't. You have the same skills to ask and connect that I do—and in case you question any of that, I'm giving you all the answers step by step. It might have taken me a long time to learn that we are not here to walk this journey alone, but once I figured that out, I invited other people along on my journey and things started changing at warp speed.

Whether you realize it or not, if you have a tribe you most likely have an undisclosed agreement with some of them. It states in invisible ink that if you start to transcend, grow, or change your beliefs, you will threaten your sense of belonging and will somehow be punished, made to feel foolish, or make people feel bad. Love may be withheld, and for some of you, extreme measures such as disowning and excommunication could be taken until you remember your place in the tribe and return safely back to acting predictably and making sure your actions and beliefs fit with theirs.

This may then lead you to think you have to "make it on your own" to make it. So you learn to fly solo in all your endeavors, and it's not easy. In fact, the first month—heck, the first week or day—of embracing a new commitment to a new goal or taking the steps to form a new habit can feel like utter torture when we don't have other people there for support and celebration. It's not impossible to go it alone, but unforeseen difficulties begin to arise after so much solo-striving. Negative feelings creep in: isolation, stress, fear of not being loved, unworthiness, exhaustion. We begin to feel misunderstood, anxious, and depressed. We might even be told by our loved ones that we think we are better than them, we are selfish, they are worried about us, or that we are no fun anymore. Spend so much time on our own island and resentment starts to build. Sure, this isolated way of getting to your goals can work—you may have even succeeded in reaching your goals; but what's the point if you can't share the happiness, the money, the promotion, the life-changing donations, the excitement, the body, or the bliss with any other soul? Success, even your biggest accomplishment, can feel lonely and exhausting. No wonder, even after some wins, feelings of confusion and rejection make their way back into your life. In time, it's easy to question if it's all worth it.

Why not quit? Just go back to how it was before. That would be easier, right? Return to whatever was half-fueling your happiness tank—the old familiar, safe job and predictable relationships. Fall back on all your temporary fixes—the happy hours, the takeout, the Netflix series, the gossip sessions. Keep the old friends, the mediocre life, and just get by. You were doing it before. Life wasn't *that* bad. Then again, life wasn't that *good* either, which is the reason your inner lioness hits you with an internal roaring temper tantrum again, because you're fed up again, which spurs you to recommit to your goals again, only to find the exact same cycle happening, again and again and again. Sound familiar? Welcome to my twenty-year cycle of Monday morning regrets.

So, then *how did I get to where I am now?*

Tribe—because you are not meant to make the big leaps alone.

Tribe moves you from transition to transcending.

WHY WOMEN THRIVE WITH TRIBE

There is evidence that the "tribe" component has actually been a part of women for a very long time. One UCLA study suggests that because of the magical combination of female reproductive hormones and oxytocin during a stressful situation, a woman is naturally hard-wired for friendship. The release of oxytocin buffers the fight-or-flight response, and pushes her to regulate her stress levels. In the distant past, this meant taking care of her children or gathering with other women. This leads to the conclusion that when "women become stressed, their inclination is to nurture those around them and reach out to others."[1] On the opposite side, men also produce oxytocin, but unlike women their hormone levels are so high that it tends to reduce the effects of it. They tend to want to be alone, flee from the stressful situation, fight back, or bottle up their feelings.[1,2]

While this is a relatively new study, the above theory may explain why women consistently outlive men. With a natural predisposition to seek the help of other women when they are feeling stressed, it's no wonder that several other studies are linking social ties to a reduction of risk for disease by lowering blood pressure, heart rate, and cholesterol. "There's no doubt," says Dr. Laura Klein, "that friends are helping us live longer."

When someone is connected to a group and feels responsibility for other people, that sense of purpose and meaning translates to taking better care of themselves.

—JULIANNE HOLT-LUNSTAD[3]

1. Randy Kamen, "A Compelling Argument About Why Women Need Friendships," *Huffington Post*, November 29, 2012, http://www.huffingtonpost.com /randy-kamen-gredinger-edd/female-friendship_b_2193062.html.

2. University of California, Los Angeles, "UCLA Researchers Identify Key Biobehavioral Pattern Used by Women to Manage Stress," *ScienceDaily*, May 22, 2000, www.sciencedaily.com/releases/2000/05/000522082151.htm.

3. J. Holt-Lunstad, T. B. Smith, and J. B. Layton, "Social Relationships and Mor-

We need groups, communities, and circles of friendship; although you might have found "your person," no one other person can be everything to another person. In fact, being solely reliant on someone else—husband, wife, partner, lover, confidant, whomever—is not only a big ask, but it puts massive stress on the relationship. It places a dangerously high expectation on both parties and it's almost guaranteed that someone is going to be let down, pushed away, or both.

Take for example, your husband. You're telling him how a coworker has been treating you unfairly. "Who cares?" he says. "Relax, she sounds like an idiot." You're a little miffed—he's supposed to be analyzing her behavior with you, figuring out what you can do or say together. Turns out, your "person" is not your best go-to person here. You're getting ready for a big work event and can't decide between two outfits, so you ask your husband what he thinks of each. "I guess the blue one is nice, but you always look good, babe." *Is that the kind of answer you wanted to hear?* No, probably not. You wanted your man to dig a little deeper with you—to choose the perfect outfit to say what you want to say with your clothes. Yeah, he's not your guy for that either. *Why?* Because most men aim to solve problems. They are not wired to hold space, to listen, to give feedback, and to analyze from all angles. No way, they want to solve whatever it is right now, and move on. Most women, however, need time to process, talk it out, and see how they feel. As opposed to men, most women do not react

---

tality Risk: A Meta-analytic Review," *PLoS Medicine* 7 (July 2010): e1000316, https://doi.org/10.1371/journal.pmed.1000316.

well when they are told what to do without being given time to figure it out.

There is a similar relationship strain if you rely only on your siblings, your children, your parent, your best friend, or your business partner to be your numero uno. Your husband might not be able to choose your perfect outfit, but he knows when you need to get to a yoga mat. Your business partner might not be able to read your moods like your husband can, but she knows you feel good giving presentations in the black jumpsuit. But it's your best friend who can tell you that you'll rock it if you wear the quartz crystal necklace she gave you and say your special prayer before you go onstage. We turn to different relationships to serve different needs. Some serve more than others, but the point is no one person is able to completely support another—no matter how much love there is. When we have a tribe we can turn to, we are able to lessen the expectation (and therefore the stress) we put on our other relationships.

TRIBAL FAIL

My first attempt at inviting people into my tribe (but I wasn't calling it a "tribe" then) was clunky. I felt like the girl everyone stared at, the girl driving around in her beat-up car covered in bumper stickers, hollering out the window from a megaphone to get the world to join her cause. "I'm looking for friends who only want to talk about deep things, scary things, real things, vulnerable things—basically everything we're not talking about." That's not only an overbearing first-time introduction in most contexts, but it scares people away. It was obvious that I needed help figuring out how to attract the people I needed and wanted into my life without freaking them out or sounding desperate. I had no idea how to create a tribe or where to begin.

I've actually gotten quite good at small talk; the trouble is, I don't like it much. It feels more to me like a juggling of chaotic energies or constantly switching partners at a hoedown rather than a good firm dance hold followed by a mesmerizing waltz. The exquisite rise and fall, underarm turns, and promenades followed by a "thank you" for that beautiful moment we shared and a goodbye when the energy has left the hold and the dance is over. In fact, there are times when small talk, "light and casual conversation about unimportant topics," as the dictionary defines it, feels so trivial that I feel physical discomfort in my body; if there is a table of food nearby, it takes all I've got to keep myself away from the nom-noms. I always seem to find myself feeding my face so I can numb-numb out and "small talk" less. But because I knew I needed to expand my network, I continued to go places and make dates to connect to new people, but after these networking events, and all the casual conversation between strangers, I still found I would leave with a full belly and an empty soul. This only confirmed why I did not go to "these types of things" in the first place. I mean, is it me, or does it get *really* old feeling like you need a *two-drink minimum* before you can spend hours talking about things that will never break the surface?

I didn't want to just take pictures together for social media to show our OOTD (outfit of the day) or that we were at an event we didn't actually have *the best time ever* at, or even a real conversation for that matter. I didn't want to talk only about the weather, their jobs, the restaurants they ate at (although I love a good restaurant, so it's not totally off the table), or what show they were binge-watching or how Instafamous someone is. "I know, I can't believe *Grey's Anatomy* is still on either . . . I love their vegan cashew kale chips . . . four million followers is amazing . . ." *and now I'm back to hitting up the cheese table on the way to the complimentary bar, on the way to the bathroom to be alone and upload my picture of me having the best time ever with people I can't be myself around.* I wanted to *know* these women. Wasn't there more to them, to us, to this new moment we were sharing? I wanted to know what their soul was whispering to them late at night, what they've been through that has made them who they are, and what makes them think the way they think. I wanted to know why they unapologetically feel proud, what they love about themselves, and what they want to contribute to the world. I wanted to know if we share the same fears, the same pasts, or even passions. I wanted to know if we could support each other's dreams! I also wanted them to know that I offered a safe place to share those dreams. But how in the world was I going to get all this across in an evening—and not sound like a nut? "Hi, I'm Lori! I'll tell you what—these tomato mozzarella skewers sure are good, but do you know what would really hit the spot? A soul-stirring conversation and an authentic connection. Tell me, what is your soul screaming at you to do and what can't you die without doing?" C'mon! I'm not alone in this feeling, am I?

I know what you're saying—"Lori, don't we have to start out with small talk to get to know each other?" My answer is yes. Most times we do need it in the beginning, but we're getting stuck in it. Hoedowns can be really fun and exciting, but they get old if you are never getting the thrill and complexity of sharing the coming together of souls in a waltz. I'm not saying that it's a good idea to go in for the conversational jugular right away or that all these networking events and small talks are negative, avoidable, or unnecessary; in fact, they can serve a great purpose—however, if this is where you go looking for some fellow soul sisters, you might find yourself in the bathroom uploading pictures, meditating, or shoving your face full of canapés. I was looking for something deeper, so I had to find my tribe a different way.

I started going to "self-help" type events hosted by various self-development powerhouses. I fell in love with the tools I was learning and the sense of freedom they were providing in my life. My goal was to learn how to put on events where women could go to find their tribe, learn these tools, and create deep connections quickly. I joined a Train the Trainer program, and as I was learning how to facilitate trainings with Jack Canfield, I couldn't ignore the concept he called "masterminding." I had heard of this before, but it only just started to resonate as I firsthand heard about how powerful this had been for him and other top transformational and business coaches. If this is what all of these people who are doing what I want to be doing are doing—why am I not doing this? Hello!!! I felt like I had unlocked the secrets of the Universe and I was getting a ginormous download that I wasn't supposed to keep this to myself—I had to start teaching all of the things that were helping me break through.

Eight months later, after every single day of using the tools I teach in this book to conquer my gut-wrenching anxiety and fear of public speaking, and wondering if I had anything useful to offer, and The Bliss Project (www.TheBlissProject.info) was born: a three-day event filled with lectures, breakout sessions, personal development exercises, yoga classes, and group meditation. An event where thousands of women were able to come together in a safe space to dive deep into their fears, get to know their soul's desires, and move through anything (or past anyone) that was holding them back with the love and support of one another. I wanted the women who attended The Bliss Project to experience all of this freeing self work and personal and professional growth, and my big dream was for them to experience all of it in the company of other soulful women.

Watching the breakthroughs these women were creating for themselves while at my events felt like the reason I was put on this planet. While many of the women reported lasting change afterward, there was still something missing. My surveys I sent after the event were telling me they didn't know how to re-create the feelings of connection and tribe that they had while at The Bliss Project. Once they got home, they felt isolated, lonely, and found it challenging to follow through on their goals they had felt so crystal clear about at the event. They began to doubt themselves and the journey even though they had felt so confident and certain. Their feelings deeply resonated with me due to my own experiences.

What happens when they go back to an environment that doesn't support these new breakthroughs? Who is going to give them all the support they need throughout this self-work process? More important, where can these women turn when they do reach their goal and end up in uncharted waters? Without a

support system, chances are, even after the most profound accomplishments, we paddle back to our island. Our island, where
it's safe, familiar, sad, and suppressed, where we know exactly
what bar has the best happy hour and exactly which bartender
will be mixing the Mai Tais, and exactly which friend is ready
to validate our sad stories while collecting paper mini umbrellas.

I didn't want these women to go back to their island. How
could I help keep them from turning back when the seas of
change got a little rough?

Once again, I was being pulled to figure out how to share
something that united women in their struggles, wins, and times
of growth that would be accessible and implemented easily into
their daily lives. It was time to share what I detected as the root
of the biggest, most accelerated learnings and miraculous blessings I had ever had in my life. I believe in my core that, just like I
was and they were, you are hungry and ready for more.

What I'm about to share with you could be the turning point
that changes everything in your journey if you're willing to stick
to it and do the work. The blessings and growth that unfolded for
me after deciding to join a tribe (we were calling it a mastermind
back then) with two other women—one I had never met in person
and barely knew from Adam—was beyond anything I could have
imagined. If I knew what was coming I would not have believed it.

TRIBE BENEFITS

So, you get it, I'm here to help you create a tribe. But what if
you're still like: *Okay, that's cool and all, but I swear I've got this
on my own.* Hey, I won't fight you. In fact, you can still read on

chapter-by-chapter and take with you all of the game-changing life lessons that I'm here to share; however, I will urge you to heavily consider the following reasons why you will greatly benefit from the deep connection that can only come from a tribe.

COMFORT: **Your tribe will help make the massive challenges feel relatively insignificant once you are comfortable sharing them within the safe space.**

Being part of a tribe means that you can vent, cry, and analyze, and you will get the support you need to help you work with the issue, the decision, or the crazy coworker at hand. You'll have accountable sisters who will keep your efforts and energy positive, focused, and *soul-ution* based. Instead of feeling beaten down, your tribe will remind you of your power, your light, your *why*, and your connection to something that's bigger than any problem.

PERSPECTIVE: **Your tribe is abundant access to wisdom in all things practical, professional, soulful, emotional, and spiritual.**

When we do this life alone it appears narrow and limited; however, when we create a tribe, we get to live out, experience, and learn the multitude of lessons and teachings that every single woman in the tribe has lived and learned. Allow other sage women, from all different walks of life, to fill you up, because once you open up to receiving all different perspectives and connections, it opens parts of you that were not accessible or flowing, and you become like a faucet that won't turn off.

VULNERABILITY: A tribe will show you the power of sharing and receiving without guilt or fear.

"Thanks for the offer but I've got this!" *Sound like you?* It sure was me. Always a giver, never a receiver. Never one to get vulnerable enough to accept help or admit I needed anything. All this lack of vulnerability did was cause me to resent everyone, because eventually people quit asking if I needed anything (because, I was always *all good*). In order to have a real connection, both parties (all parties) must not only be vulnerable enough to give wholeheartedly but also to receive wholeheartedly.

ACCOUNTABILITY: Your tribe will hold you to the flame.

We need people who can call us out on our behavior. These are the women who keep you in check when you start believing your negative stories, when you start giving in to your fear, and when you start to justify your own excuses. If you're playing small, they will hold up that mirror to show the truth. If you're complaining or having trouble moving past something, in a loving way your tribe will help guide you to understand what the root of the issue is and what you could do to create a different outcome.

CONFIDENCE: Your tribe will help you move forward even in the face of fear, uncertainty, and judgment.

Most of us need to be pushed out of the plane. It's easy to say we're going skydiving. It's easy to plan and pay for a trip to go skydiving, but how easy is it when it comes time to jump out of the plane? Um, it's not. It's terrifying. Welcome to every big decision. But your tribe will gently nudge (or aggressively push if needed) you right out of that tiny plane door into the free fall, reminding you that anything worth doing is tough and scary.

I am everything because of my tribe. When the shame from a failure or fear of the future tries to swallow me whole or tells me it's not worth it and to close off my heart again, they speak life into me. A tribe says "me too, stay open or get up and try again" and suddenly you're not alone and the feelings loosen their death grip. Knowing that I have a tribe that has my back has allowed me to take more risks and bigger leaps, because no matter what, I have my people who accept me unconditionally, and I them. And, my friend, when you have that, you are unstoppable.

four

WHAT IS STOPPING US?

How we're attempting to connect and communicate woman-to-woman is working about as well as searching for fudge brownies in a steaming cow pie. There are definitely goddesses waiting to elevate with you, as you are already learning, but unchecked emotions, lack of boundaries, fear of rejection, and need for acceptance are turning how we communicate into a shit show. It just all feels so messy and complicated, but it doesn't have to be that way.

Your depth of connection will depend on your willingness to *try on* new ideas. Look, it's not always going to be easy and you're probably not going to like some of the things I have to say, but I'm not here to be that friend who sugarcoats everything— that gets you nothing but a stomachache and muffin top, and ain't nobody got time for that. I'm here for your breakthrough and bliss—that means it's going to cost you your temporary comforts, possibly some relationships, and most definitely your old life.

Earlier I shared what I felt like before I had a tribe, but I wanted to really take the pulse of the women in some of my social networks outside of my tribe. So, I went straight to the place where people seem to love to share, well, everything . . . and I reached out to Facebook-land and posed a question. The post said, "I'm doing some book research and I would adore your help if this applies to you: What are some of the reasons why you don't feel connected to women, have women friends, or feel you can't connect deeply with women? Please be as honest as possible!" I came back an hour later to hundreds of comments. It wasn't just a few words but it was paragraphs about the issues they have with women, how they see other women, and the pain they feel around the subject of having close women friends. It was like a volcano of pain was finally allowed to erupt.

The post is still going as I write this chapter, because despite feeling "desperate" for deeper connection as most of them stated, we are fear-stricken by the thought of it for a plethora of reasons (we'll cover those in a bit). In fact, we're so fear-stricken that many said they had "sworn off having women friends." I could so relate, and this broke my heart . . . The truth is, I felt overwhelmed by the answers at first, and even recently had an undesirable experience that made me question my female relationships for a hot second before coming back to the tools I'm going to share with you.

Tears filled my eyes in the coffee shop as I consumed and felt each and every word. I looked up from my computer to see four very well-put-together women sitting alone, typing away, taking breaks from what appeared to be work to scroll on their phones. On the surface they appeared to have it all together, but I wondered if deep down (or not so deep down) they had the same struggles? I couldn't help but think that these women are the same women leaving the comments on my post. We've become masters of being "fine," and if loneliness strikes we will just get another hit from digital narcotics in efforts to numb the phantom pain of our self-amputated limb of sisterhood. It's easier to pretend it was never a part of who we were to begin with. Ms. Independent gets all the accolades . . . and celebrates it *ALONE*.

My excitement about this book comes from my highest intention and ancient feminine desire (I know you feel it too) for more of us to re-enroll in our tribal roots so we can create a movement, or more like, restore faith so we can once again become what we fundamentally were born to be, a unit working as one—not one burning the candle at both ends trying to be everything alone.

My goal is to get this book into the hands of women willing to step in and become a Tribe Leader of this *new way* of being, belonging, and connecting, regardless of past beliefs or fear, so together we can patch the fabric that has been torn apart and remember the golden thread of sisterhood that binds us to our most colossal power, prowess, and potential of all . . . our *Bliss Tribe*—our quilted blanket of solace, our place of growth, safety, restoring, and recharging.

We stop our natural inclination to connect by second guessing a compliment to another woman, worried she may think we're weird, or returning our gaze to the safety of our phone when we actually wanted to smile and share a conversation. It's time to rise up and it begins by looking up and seeing each other for what we really are. Humans. Sisters. One.

Let's take some sisterly inventory, shall we? You may be able to relate to one or all of these. I know I certainly recalled my old stories when I read these. Here's how we currently feel about each other and why we can't seem to connect. Which ones are you?

Maybe you feel like:

Women are so catty.
Women are mean.
Women are dramatic.
Women are competitive.
Women are jealous.
Women are too emotional.
Women gossip too much.
Women worry too much about what others think.
Women are intimidated by me.
Women are needy.
Women are judgmental.
Women friends are energy vampires.

Or maybe you've said:

I don't trust women.
I get along better with guys.
I give too much and it never gets reciprocated.
I don't care about clothes, hair, and makeup.
I can't talk about kids all day.
I turn into their therapist.
I don't want to always go out drinking.
I hate the phone.
I'm an introvert.

I'm always disappointed by women friendships.

There is no spark or energy there.

I can't find any like-minded women.

I'm geographically isolated.

I don't have time for friends.

I have nothing to offer the women I want to be friends with.

I'm too jealous to be friends with women I find interesting.

I'm too ashamed to share myself and my story with friends.

I'm not willing to go through the pain of getting hurt or rejected again.

The list keeps going. Far too many open wounds for all of us to lick, but we can start with the ones we have control over: our own.

five

BUILD YOUR TRIBE

In everyone's life, at some time, our inner fire goes out. It is then burst into flame by an encounter with another human being. We should all be thankful for those people who rekindle the inner spirit.

—ALBERT SCHWEITZER

HOW TO BUILD YOUR BLISS TRIBE

In this chapter, I am going to teach you how to create your Bliss Tribe. Then, once your tribe is formed, we—you, me, and your tribe—are going to go through the curriculum together. You will decide when and how often you want to connect to discuss the chapters and Soul Assignments you did on your own, what discoveries you made or what came up for you. There are *Soul Assignments* and *Tribe Work*. *Soul Assignments* are done on your own after reading the chapter on your own, and the *Tribe Work* is done only during your chosen *Bliss Tribe Meeting* times.

Don't stress if this sounds like a lot of work right now; I've laid this book out so you can take it one step at a time. The benefits that come from the little work involved will help you accomplish all your goals and back you up with loving support. When you use this book, exactly as suggested, you, too, will create a safe and sacred space, where you can share and connect on a soul level with other women.

All you have to do is show up and do the work suggested.

NOTE: *If you're not ready to do this as a tribe yet, and still want to use this book as an epic self-development journey, then skip to section 2, chapter 7, page 89. You can always come back and assemble your tribe later!*

THE NUTS AND BOLTS OF TRIBE

A tribe consists of three or more people who come together, either in person, via computer, or over the phone, to discuss, brainstorm, create, solve, and elevate each other's lives, all bound by a verbal confidentiality agreement.

Tribes become extremely actionable as a result of the strong bond formed between members of the group. Nothing that is said in the group will ever be shared with anyone outside of the group (unless specific permission is given). When members of the tribe commit to being open, honest, and accountable with each other, the acceleration of individual growth for each member is powerful. You are welcome to share as much or as little as you like with your tribe, but know that the most growth comes from being vulnerable when you are ready. Listen—I'm not saying this model is 100 percent foolproof and your first efforts at tribe are going to score you pure bliss, but it's pretty damn close. The women who truly commit to this type of structured accountability and don't flake usually have your best interest at heart. That's not to say a few unripened apples (not so awakened) can't slip through the cracks, make it into your tribe, and bring up those old stories, because I've definitely been blindsided and had a tribe fall apart because they broke trust and commitments. Part of your bliss and tribe work is to learn how to handle it, move through the hurt, and see the lesson it offered you. Look at it like dating: we don't decide to be celibate because of a few bad relationships. They just get you clearer on what you are looking for and what you will and won't tolerate. Even if it's your default response, don't close off your heart—promise me you will stay open to the abundant blessings that will come if you keep trying at this—which we will also discuss.

Below are the principles to set up your mastermind, and if you do as suggested—from magic numbers to tribal rules—you will have an effective and actionable Bliss Tribe.

THE MAGIC NUMBER

Three to four people. A tribe operates best when it is no fewer than three people and no more than four people. Two people limits perspective, feedback, and the number of different ideas. More than four, and the group begins to feel less intimate and people end up scrambling over time to share. There are some exceptions if you meet for longer periods of time or less often. In this case a bigger number of five women or more could work because everyone will have adequate time to share. Twenty minutes a person seems to be the sweet spot that allows the type of connection I talk about in this book.

THE DREAM PEOPLE

Absolutely anyone. This is your opportunity to invite anyone you would like to connect with, learn from, and share your time with to join your tribe. You can ask absolutely anyone. There is no stipulation here. You can go the familiar route with the people you know—your family, coworkers, acquaintances, best friends, or workout buddies. Or another option is to take the fast-track growth route by choosing people you don't actually know too well—people who come from different industries, backgrounds, or beliefs. I've learned that the more diverse your tribe, the more growth potential you have, because any time you seek people who are outside of your comfort zone—people doing something that you want to start doing, people who hold strengths that you don't possess—you will stretch faster and further. In fact, most all of my tribes began with people I barely knew, if at all. I basically knew they were driven, seemed caring, and wanted to grow. But, no matter which people you choose to invite, be sure that you consider each one of them reliable and goal-oriented individuals. You will become strong and action-oriented only when everyone contributes and shares equally.

THE CONSISTENT TRIBE MEETING

You can meet weekly or biweekly (every two weeks). How often is your choice, but the key is consistency—for my tribe, biweekly is what works best to stay consistent and weekly was too much. Try to schedule meetings at the same time—same day, same hour. What else is a key factor to success? Never meet for longer than one hour. Be strict about this, and do not go over this allotted time unless it has been discussed and agreed upon by the entire group prior to the meeting. The Time Keeper (more on that duty below) will keep everyone on track so that each person present gets the same amount of minutes to talk and feel heard. You might think an hour is not that long, but if you're consistent in your meetings it's just right and keeps this meet-up from becoming a burden or something to resent.

THE EFFECTIVE INVITE

Formally ask people to join your tribe. Nervous? Not sure how to go about asking people to join your tribe? I've got a script you can use below or you can purchase the book for your tribe and fill out the official *A Tribe Called Bliss* Invite in the beginning of the book. Please tweak and personalize the script below as needed, but I'm sharing it with you because this is a general idea of what works for me when reaching out to women I want to connect with. Just don't be afraid to ask. The worst thing that can happen is someone says no, but remember that just opens space for someone else.

Hey _____

*How are you? I think you are amazing and I would love
to get to know you better, share goals, and see how we
can support each other. I'm contacting you because I just
purchased a book called* A Tribe Called Bliss *that is based on
the shared interest of women supporting women. I am putting
together a small group of women, and we will be using this
book as a guide. If you are craving support, connection,
feedback, and real conversation at a soul level, I would love
to have you join us.*

*If you want to be a part of the tribe I'm starting, I'll send
you details. It would be a short commitment, most likely an
hour every two weeks, and we will all respect the clock and
each other's schedules! Just know I admire all you do and think
you would be a valuable addition to this group.*

Looking forward to hearing back either way!

XX
Lori

THE TRIBE WORK (GROUP WORK)

Assign homework. Prior to meeting each time, decide what chapters the group will read and what Soul Assignments to complete. For example, your first email could read like this:

Hello, Bliss Tribe!

*Welcome to week one of our first official Bliss Tribe meeting!
Up to this point you should have chapters one through six
read to understand the structure and flow. I know some
serious magic is about to happen. Thank you for saying yes!
Please make sure you keep this date, as it is important to each
member.*

When:
   *Thursday, 8:00 AM (PST) via Skype, phone, or in person.
   Please be sure to respond with your Skype IDs and
   phone numbers if applicable.*

This Week's Jobs:
   Tribe Leader/Time Keeper: [name]
   Sacred Space Creator: [name]
   [Roles described below]

This Week's Assignment:
   *Read chapters one–six & complete all Soul Assignments
   on your own. Be prepared to partake in the tribe discussion.*
   [Note: There are no Soul Assignments on your first meeting. It
   will just be a list of questions to bond your tribe that you will all
   be answering. You will be given those directions in chapter six.]

Some Tips:
   *It helps for everyone involved to keep a running journal
   to document the date and whose turn it is each week for*

each job and also what everyone is working on so we can
hold each other accountable the next week.

Remember, every week is different and we will have
our ups and downs and this is about love, support, and
showing up no matter how bad we want to quit or make
excuses.

Talk to you all soon!

XX
Lori

THE TRIBE JOBS

Get ready, because we are taking your tribal "roles" seriously.
Each meeting, tribe members will take turns rotating between
two different roles—*The Tribe Leader* and *The Sacred Space
Creator*. All extra members are just participants that week. Because the roles rotate every meeting, everyone will take equal
turns having a "free" week with no role other than participant.
When everyone keeps to their appointed roles, time will not be
wasted, sharing and goals will stay on track, and all members of
the tribe will flourish.

THE TRIBE LEADER: She sends the reminder email that
week to each person, initiates the call, opens the meeting, keeps
the time, and introduces the topic and the homework related to
the meeting's agenda. Throughout the meeting, she prompts the
group with questions and discussion related to the content of
the meet-up, and when it's time to finish, she wraps up quickly
by saying *"Thank you all so much for sharing yourselves and
your truth with us today,"* then states who is leading the next

call. The Tribe Leader also officially ends the call by hanging up and disconnecting.

Tribe Leader Tips:

Opening Language:

> *"Hello, everyone! Let's get started right away.* [No small talk ever beforehand.] *It looks like this week's jobs are* [go over who is assigned to each job this week]. *Now, let's have* [Sacred Space Creator] *say the prayer."*

After Prayer (to prompt first participant to share):

> *"What's been coming up for you after completing* [the assigned chapter]? *And let us know if you want some input at the end so I can prompt you to finish up in order to leave a few minutes."*

Closing Language (after all have shared):

> *"Hey, ladies, out of respect for everyone's schedule, we are out of time. Feel free to send the group an email with your closing thoughts if you don't feel complete. Have an amazing weekend, and looking forward to connecting soon!"*

As the Tribe Leader, you are also the Time Keeper: Your job is of TOP importance for this meeting to run smoothly. You must be able to interject in a loving way, because timing is paramount in giving everyone equal opportunity to share and contribute. You must speak up and give warnings at the two-minute mark. In doing so, the Time Keeper ends the current conversation in a loving manner so the group can move on to the next person's turn to share. Remember, the Time Keeper's job is to keep it sweet and simple.

Suggested Time Keeper Language:

At the two-minute mark you say:

"Thank you so much for sharing and it's your two-minute warning. What could we help with to make you feel complete and keep you accountable until next time?"

When the tribe member's time is up:

"Thank you so much for sharing. It's time to move on to the next member."

or:

"Your time has come to a close and it is time to move on. Feel free to journal your final thoughts for next week or email for closure."

THE SACRED SPACE CREATOR: This role follows the Tribe Leader's welcome with a few words of prayer or gratitude. This job is vital and gets the group present, grounded, and open to give and receive from a place of the highest good. This is an important part of the meet-up, because everyone will be coming off busy schedules and agendas and will need to release the "busy." It is of utmost importance you welcome-in a higher presence to help guide feelings and thoughts to open the tribe up to new possibilities and support. Even if this isn't your jam, try it out. You may be surprised. If nothing else, there is no harm done. If you're not sure of what to say as a Sacred Space Creator, you can use, tweak, or get inspired by the following script.

Sacred Space Creator Tips:

Example Prayer:

> *"We ask that [holy spirit/God/love/energy] be present in this gathering to help us get grounded and present with each other and guide us with the intention of the highest good for all. We ask to be open to all possibilities and resolutions coming from the utmost place of love. We ask for strength to release and forgive anything that is blocking us and achieve our highest personal and spiritual potential by discovering and using our unique gifts holding the intention of elevating the planet. We know that there is nothing that will come our way for which we would not be given the courage and resources to move through."*

[Closing of your choosing, such as Amen/Namaste/with Love, let's begin.]

THE MEETING FLOW

Consistency and equality. Keep these two things in mind for every single meeting. As noted above, I believe an hour is plenty of time for a mastermind or meet-up if you are meeting biweekly, so let's look at what a one-hour flow would look like.

Opening Time: *3 minutes*

Keep it short and sweet. The Leader welcomes, keeps time, sets the tone, and the Sacred Space Creator reinforces the safe space to share.

Tribe Discussion Time: *varies, depending on the number of people in the tribe*

Say there are four members in the tribe. Each person would get 13 minutes. Say there are three members, the Soul Share time increases to 18 minutes.

Closing Time: *2 minutes*

The Tribe Leader closes the meeting in under two minutes with reminders of the next meeting time, assignments, and jobs and disconnects call.

Feedback Time: *Each member must announce before their turn if they know they want feedback on something from the tribe. This is included as part of their allotted*

*time. Do not go over another member's allotted time for
any reason.*

It is important to allow all parties time to give input—and
please be aware that many of us are not coaches. It's important
to ask questions or offer a perspective that helps another person
to come up with their own answers. We are not here to tell each
other what to do. We are just holding the space and listening so
that person is able to come to their own conclusion. Here's an
example of a questions that I love to ask:

*"If you could ask your heart from a place of love what you
should do, what do you think that would be?"*

"Is there a choice that feels more aligned than the other?"

"Does it bring you joy?"

"How does that make you feel?"

THE TRIBAL RULES

Respect your group.

That's why I've created these rules and guidelines and time
frames. Without them, it's easy to lose the power of what you
are creating. Not only that, those who are high performers
will want to leave if the rules and respect are compromised. *A
Tribe Called Bliss* is for people who are ready and willing to
take this commitment on, which means showing up, doing the
work, and respecting time. The top reasons tribes fall apart
are people not showing up, rescheduling, and not respecting
boundaries and time.

Stick with it.

At first, this commitment to a book and a tribe might feel completely foreign, even a bit uncomfortable. I get it. I was there. It felt weird and challenging and I didn't always feel like I had anything to say at first or anything to offer! At times you don't want to show up—you'd rather be doing something else, anything else. You might even fight with yourself about why you are doing this. When it gets tough, do your best to stick with it and navigate the feelings and challenges that may come up. Remember that discomfort is gifted to us to help us grow and to learn more lessons. We show up to get stronger, love harder, and be greater. We show up because we decide that we want to be the type of person that shows up for ourselves and the people who are important to us, because when we do this, they can do the same for us. We show up because it is what we do. In time, this will become one of the single best gifts you have ever received.

Be patient.

Stay in it long enough to feel the transformation, because forming this group can be the most transformative thing you ever do. Not only is it a commitment to show up, but it introduces the vulnerability of sharing and the accountability of being there for others. It will take your life and your goals to another level. Soon, you will move through feelings quicker, dissolve issues faster, and connect deeper. You will begin to take more risks because you know you are being supported in a way you have never experienced.

Big shifts do not happen overnight, but soon you will find the kind of tribe and conversation that makes you forget there's food and wine at the party and makes you wish you didn't have to pee . . . when's the last time you had a conversation like that? Mine was a few days ago. We joked about wearing diapers the next time we got together so we didn't have to leave the conversation we were feasting on, even for a minute.

You can use this simple chapter-by-chapter structure until your group has read all of *A Tribe Called Bliss* and completed and discussed the chapter exercises. Feel free to do more than one chapter at a time if it works better for the group. However, once you have gone through the whole book, I highly suggest reading another book of this kind and asking what came up after each chapter using this format. Or simply keep up the regular meetings without the book with this tribe, and continue to discuss and celebrate goals, create action plans, and work through whatever is coming up over that course of time.

IT'S TIME TO BUILD YOUR TRIBE

It's time to get the ball rolling, get the party started, get the spark ignited. It's time to send out invitations. Refer to the Invite section of this book or copy and paste from www.atribecalledbliss.com and send. Even if the answer is no, accept the response lovingly and move on to the next. It's all perfect so trust that.

No matter who you decide to ask to join your Bliss Tribe, make sure to get a firm commitment that they will plan to be there no matter what. Okay, sure, life happens, and people will run into situations that they cannot avoid, but ask that they let the group know as early as possible when they absolutely cannot make it. You might be able to reschedule for a new time that works for all; however, word of caution here: Constant rescheduling can cause a tribe to fall apart. To avoid the scheduling pitfall, create a firm agreement that clarifies why you are all here. Being a member of your tribe is not only about showing up for yourself and your goals, but also about showing up for each other and everyone else's goals. Commitment to yourself and the group are mutually important. You show up—at all times. You show up for the love and support, and you show up when the goal-ing gets tough.

Two things to be aware of.

No one can invite anyone in without passing it by each other. In fact, if you have a tribe that works well, I would recommend NOT inviting any more people that throw off the timing and flow unless you all agree it would be a great value! This will be tempting, to want to add more people, but this may be a calling for you to help them create their group instead. I recommend teaching that other person how to build their own tribe, and then maybe you all can meet in person once a year or whatever works for the majority!

Once in a great while some people may not be a fit for the group. Most often it's because they are not willing to do the work to move through a problem, they are showing up to each meeting negative, or they are not respecting the tribe rules. Usually these people tend to separate themselves, but if not, sometimes you will have to lovingly remind them of the things they agreed on when coming in, and if it's not a fit and they are not keeping their word you may have to say, it's just not right for the group at this time and you appreciate them giving it a try. It's not easy, but this is not about complaining or coddling . . . these are the agreements and rules for a stellar group that is committed to solutions and goals, and all are accountable to each other and themselves.

six

YOUR FIRST MEETING

I have a belief that if we don't have the tribe and relationships we want it's not because we can't find the right people, it's because we're afraid of real connection. We are afraid of the work it takes. We are afraid of how we show up or of not offering enough value in relationships. We're also afraid to ask deeper questions in order to move past the small talk—even scarier, what do we say if we do get past the small talk? Will we be accepted if we can't yet accept ourselves for exactly how and where we are? We keep it superficial because we don't know what to ask and we fear being intrusive or being rejected. In life, if you want more engaging answers, you need to ask more thought-provoking questions, so wouldn't this also be true for wanting more soulful connections? The answer is yes! If you want more meaningful relationships, you need to ask deeper, more personal questions; also go in search of the answers to these questions for yourself so you can be prepared for the fire and transformation that happen past the surface. But how do we know the right context for asking such questions?

The desire is there, but many of us don't have the practice, the know-how, or the right questions that would help us create the type of connections we're craving with others and ourselves. Even if you do, you don't know how to approach the person to create a safe space that would hold the type of relationship you are actually desiring. I felt the exact same way for longer than I would like to admit. This is one of the biggest reasons I knew I had to write this book. We make it so much harder than it has to be—not anymore!

Before my speaking events, I always ask people what they are seeking to achieve. Among the top three things they list is always to feel a sense of tribe, deeper self-awareness, and to leave with real connections and friends. This got me to thinking what the quickest way to create this was when sometimes I only have an hour or, at best, three days at an event. I was aware they were not going to get this just from coming and sitting next to someone, mingling, and making small talk. I had to learn how to create a space safe enough for two or more strangers to dive into conversations that they may never have with even the people closest to them . . .

How the hell can I have these people create that type of bond with each other in such a short amount of time? The answer is giving people who have a mutually vested interest in creating deeper bonds and exploring self-awareness a safe, sacred space and a format that is easy to follow.

When I started to research more on quickly creating close connections, I found this experiment that describes exactly what we were doing in these "group circles" at my events and in my mastermind groups, and this is why people were leaving with the tribes and connections they wanted.

Social psychologist Arthur Aron created a study titled "The Experimental Generation of Interpersonal Closeness: A Procedure and Some Preliminary Findings." The researchers were seeking to discover if they could "create closeness in a reasonably short amount of time." They conceived a list of thirty-six questions designed to simplify things and help people get to know each other quickly. Talking of the study, Aron explains, "The questions gradually get more and more personal, so they begin with questions that are almost small talk and then they move to talk about some of the deepest, most intimate things in your life, and they almost always make two people feel better about each other and want to see each other again."

This exercise is based off this idea of creating close connections quickly, and when we do these circles of question, answer, and discussion at my events, afterward I always ask a question: "Who feels closer to this group of strangers than they do with most of the friends in their lives?"

I am always astounded by the fact that almost the entire room raises their hands . . . All we did was ask more quality questions and take turns answering and listening. The connections they created are exactly what you're about to create in this exercise.

I came up with new questions to do something similar, but also to help you move toward your bliss and become more self-aware. I've used most of these questions at my events, so I know this works. Don't stress—you only have to get as personal as you're comfortable with. You are not forced to do anything, but if you are willing to get uncomfortable, you have more opportunity to feel more connected than if you didn't—remember, you've all agreed to create a sacred, safe place and respect each other's privacy, so keep the answers to yourself unless they say something different.

These questions are intended for your first tribe meeting, but these are also amazing for creating closer connections with anyone in your life.

YOUR FIRST MEETING

This will be the only meeting that I recommend meeting for 90 minutes to two hours if possible. It is vital that you get to know each other and bond your group before moving forward and getting into the work of the book.

This will work similarly to your other meetings, but before you begin remember you are responsible for creating and keeping this a safe and sacred space—that means releasing judgment of yourself and others, following the tribe rules, keeping this conversation within your tribe only, and calling upon the highest compassion and truth to help guide each person into their own answers. Please do not interrupt or fill the space while others are talking. If you are asked for feedback, don't make it about you or your opinion, instead keep a series of solution-based questions for them in mind. Simply learn to hold the space, be loving and calm so each person can fully express and move through emotions.

Tribe Discussion:

The first member whose turn it is to share begins by saying the questions out loud and then immediately answering them. Try to get through all the questions in the time allotted if possible.

When their time is up, the Tribe Leader interjects and moves on
to the next member to then do the same.

Tell us a little bit about yourself.

Why are you excited to have a tribe?

What are five things you're grateful for right now?

What feels fun for you right now?

What is not fun for you?

*Where are you getting the most fulfillment from right
    now?*

What's draining you the most?

*Do you have any secret passions you would like to
    pursue? What are they and why?*

What are you most excited about in your life right now?

What are you most nervous about or what scares you?

What are your strengths?

Where do you struggle the most right now?

What are three things you're proud of about yourself?

What's missing in your life right now?

*Complete this sentence: If you really knew me you
    would know that . . .*

REMINDER:

Don't forget to set the appointment for your next tribe meeting
and choose what chapter or chapters you will discuss next. (Suggestion: Continue on to read the next section introduction and
chapter 7 on your own and complete the Soul Assignment, but
wait to do the Tribe Work together during your next meeting.)

section two

THE NEW WAY
OF BEING

7 SACRED AGREEMENTS

Welcome to section two: "The New Way of Being." When I say "being" it's not just about what you are doing or saying, but the intention and feeling you're holding when you're doing and saying it. It's about how you make people feel and what energy you are holding while walking through life and sending out into the world. Here begins the warrior-level work of being the nonjudgmental observer of the outcome of the way you have been "being." This self-awareness and ownership over how you're "being" is what will finally create serious change and lasting connection.

In this section you are going to learn and understand the seven sacred agreements of the New Way of Being that are going to move you through the blocks, stories, and beliefs that used to stop you from supporting yourself, reaching your goals, and being a part of a sisterhood. This is the new language and set of agreements between yourself and your tribe that will finally incite and allow real, lasting connection. In this section you will be implementing the new tribe format, going through each chapter on your own, and then discussing it with your tribe at your scheduled meeting.

THE SEVEN SACRED AGREEMENTS OF THE NEW WAY OF BEING

I think it's pretty obvious that we need a new girl code. Not only a new way of being and perceiving each other, but ourselves as well. These next seven agreements are pertinent to your bliss and having a lasting Bliss Tribe because the extent of our dreams and relationships can't go beyond the ceiling of our mindset. You'll only go as far as you're willing to grow. These agreements will help you move through everything you will encounter individually and within your tribe.

Remember, every relationship has unspoken agreements we adhere to when we decide to form any type of bond. We assume everyone holds the same agreements as we do, except due to past events, beliefs, and upbringing they NEVER do. When something goes unspoken, it will eventually be broken—not maliciously, but because there's an unstated expectation and lack of clear communication. This ends up in false stories, hurt feelings, and distrust. We need a set of agreements that state from the beginning what you desire, expect, and need from the connection in order to make it last, and also a code of conduct for when times get tough—because they will. This is important because we may feel we are not bound to our tribe anymore. We can just leave and go back to a less complicated version of what wasn't working because it wasn't working—"just fine." But, this is where our entire life gets stuck, this is where we keep settling for less. How you react and act in your tribe is how you act and react everywhere in your life. Stop settling for mediocre when you're the furthest thing from it.

In order to have grounded, meaningful tribes of women, or any relationship for that matter, we are going to have to challenge the status quo of what we have learned through history about ourselves and each other. We are not just fighting for us, but every single woman who has been stripped of her well-being, peace of mind, trust, self-worth, and power because of old beliefs—women are evil, less than, competitive, needy, and can't be trusted. When we continue buying into these ideas, we continue to willfully give our power away. If you want better, brighter, more brilliant lives, friendships, and futures for our daughters and the world, it has to begin with you. Don't you dare look left or right, you are THE one who will make this change. You are made from Source Energy and your time to rise is now. I know you feel it. Your life will mean something. You will not die with your highest self still trapped inside of you. Suit up, sister, we're headed into the arena—together.

I was raised to never hurt anyone's feelings, to be there for everyone, and to go out of my way to make people comfortable even if that meant sacrificing my ideas, desires, personal time, and opinions. It was all about making sure people liked me and that my reputation was pure and in good standing—not so easy when you're a human. Many women I talk to were raised to be on the lookout for backstabbing women or to compare themselves or attack the "enemy," aka any woman who has what you want. We've learned that if we want friends who love us, it's going to cost us our time, energy, peace of mind, health, identity, and possibly our pocketbook, if like me you thought you could buy people's affection. In a nutshell, this is gonna hurt. It's time to let go of archaic ideas and let our hearts take the wheel. They've known all along what's best.

I know the thought of tribe and female relationships may be causing a panic attack at this very moment. I get it, the pain runs deep, thousands of years to be exact. You've been hurt, bored to tears, annoyed, bullied, even tortured. But although it feels like you're protecting yourself or you're better off, you are missing out on a sisterhood that would enhance your life. Look, I can't promise you that you won't get hurt again, but I will tell you that if you build enough like-minded tribes and follow this new code, you will be able to unlock an entirely new part of your soul that brings the fulfillment, richness, and perspective that you've been missing. You may even thank the fallouts for bringing you to an entirely new level, teaching you lessons you will need moving forward.

When I say sisterhood, you may picture a group of women dancing in dresses and braiding each other's hair. Full honesty, that would have scared the living bejesus out of me back in the day, and for many of you, that sounds like crap and a total waste of time. Maybe your tribe will look like that if you want it to— I know one of mine does—or maybe it will be the ultimate conversation about business, life, and slaying your goals with fierce boundaries and refreshing honesty! Just like everything in life, it will be whatever you decide to create for yourself—I just urge you to stay open, dancing and all. I've got every type of tribe now . . . because I am all of it. I will never have just one tribe with one set of ideas. I am multifaceted and my tribes need to reflect that. I don't want them to be all butterflies. I want them to challenge me to look at my beliefs, think bigger, love harder, and grow. That way when you are in different seasons of your life, you have tribes that hold that space for you and give support and perspective.

I'm feeling that old familiar feeling that comes right before a colossal breakthrough. I imagine it's how John Candy felt while sitting in front of "The Old Ninety-Sixer" from *The Great Outdoors*, sweating about taking down the overwhelmingly massive steak, but like anything else . . . WE are going to do this one bite at a time.

Let me introduce you to your new girl code. No, I'm not going to tell you some editorial magazine crap about how rule number one is to not sleep with your best friend's ex—even though this is useful if you had this happen to you or vice versa. Instead, think don Miguel Ruiz's "Four Agreements": four rules that help you lead an exceptional life, and apply to anything—but specifically to women and to those building a tribe. These are your seven guiding principles you can always come back to when things feel like they are spinning out of control or challenges arise in your life or in your tribes. Throughout the next seven chapters we are going to dive into each one in detail.

seven

AGREEMENT 1: ALWAYS BE YOUR OWN GURU

There I was in another self-development training. I had logged hundreds of hours at "like" events at this point, and despite knowing my soul's calling as a speaker and spiritual teacher, I still didn't feel ready to go out and teach this stuff on my own. We were thirty minutes submerged into a profound visualization where we were guided in our mind to a secret garden to meet a sage Goddess who we could choose to represent Mother Earth, The Divine, an angel, or a guide of some sort. We were told she held an ornate box that possessed the final gift that we needed to feel ready to step into our sanctified mission on this planet. We were to know that whatever we received in the box was our soul's way of signifying and gifting us everything we needed to move forward into our calling.

My moment of truth was finally here. I knew that this was

the missing puzzle piece in my journey and exactly what I needed to finally be anointed ready and worthy to step into my dream. Everything was going swimmingly. I was so consumed by the power of this visualization that I actually felt like I had directly connected with Source. It was my time to open my gift box . . .

In my magic garden that I created, next to a river, my sturdy grandfather tree and my feet in the most lush, pillow-soft green moss, I stand before my Angel Goddess with long, liquid silver hair and white flowing garments. I lean in to open the ornately decorated box. I do this slowly because I want to savor and honor this moment for its significance, and suddenly, I lean in, ready to feel worthy and confident to begin my mission . . . I realize the box is empty. *WTF?! Okay, it's okay, Lori, just close the box and try again . . . it's your visualization—you got this*, I think to myself. So that's what I do. I close the box and reopen it for the next five minutes. Nothing, nada, big fat zilcho. *This bitch is not delivering!! I need this gift! C'mon, lady—give it up! I can't reach my calling if I can't make anything show up in this box!* Still empty. *Look, I'm sorry I called you a bitch. It's just that I've been at this for so long and I know I'll feel ready if you could just show me what's in the damn box.*

After the visualization ended, we all shared as a group what we saw in our box and what we learned with the group. Everyone was raising their hand and sharing how they got something so fucking spectacular that helped represent their gifts and the power they are meant to share and now they're ready to take on the world! While I'm over here thinking, *Wow, I'm so happy for you guys . . . I'll just keep waiting with my empty-ass box while you go live your dreams.* I refused to settle for an empty box and a visualization that didn't work, so I raised my hand to let him know something went wrong with my visualization. "What do you do if your box is empty? My box was empty. Everything was great and felt amazing and then my box was empty. This didn't work for me," I said. "Everyone got exactly what they needed," our facilitator replied with a grin. I was not satisfied with that idiotic answer, but I fake-smiled and sat down nodding my head with a confused look on my face and started to think. I wanted someone to tell me what I needed! I wanted so badly for someone to anoint me, give me the answers, and tell me I'm ready!

Later that day I realized that was the best gift I have ever gotten—the box full of nothing and the lack of answers. It was my perfect gift that I now see was precisely what I needed. I didn't need anything. I already had everything inside of me. I finally understood after taking the time to get quiet that no amount of courses, books, education, or validation from others was going to make me feel ready to share my gifts until I believed I could trust myself and that I was enough no matter what anyone else does or says. We anoint ourselves when we take the first step with the fear and doubt. Holy shit! This really works! I'm ready! I was in tears, I felt this on such a deep soul level that I had a glimpse of my unshakable and totally accessible faith. We always know even when we feel we don't. We're just listening to the noise of other people's fears, looking in all the wrong places and not slowing down long enough to tune into what our voice and feelings are trying to tell us.

What I want to make clear is that I believe in whatever type of guide helps you on your path. They are vital to learn from and gain knowledge. I have had more guidance and mentors than I can count and still do! I have a carved wooden statue of Oprah, whom I ask for guidance every day—kidding, but don't put it past me. There is a difference between taking everything they say for gospel, never making a decision without them, and asking for guidance, then making sure you give yourself some time to check in to see if it feels aligned before making any big decisions— after all, these are humans who are just doing the best they can from their own experiences and aren't perfect as well. The main reasons we give all of our power and decision making over to a coach, our parents, partner, teachers, friends—you name it—is because we aren't ready to fully take ownership of our choices and the current reality they created. It's easier to blame someone else who told you what to do than to own the responsibility of your actions and your situation. Ultimately relying on your intuition and ability to feel what's right for you will sharpen the more you use it. Wayne Dyer says "When you trust in yourself, you trust in the very wisdom that created you." If you're looking for a guide besides yourself, use the one who refers back to you and leads you to your own answers. They will ask the right questions that empower you to use your own voice, they will celebrate a choice that feels right for you even if it's opposite of theirs, and they will always remind you to come back to love and check in with your inner guide.

In the beginning, teachers and coaches are a huge help, especially if you can't hear that voice yet. One thing you can do to really use them effectively is check in with how you feel after you read, meet, or chat with them. Do you feel uplifted or like your highest intentions are being looked after? Do you leave with good feelings around people in your life, or do you feel heavy, gross, or like you need a shower? Do you feel you can disagree freely and ask questions?

I've learned no matter how right or wrong a life or business decision goes, I am the only one who can create my bliss, find my lesson, and choose my blessing in all of it. With that said, I know my teachers are human and I release them from being perfect. I choose what advice and teachings work in my life and I leave what isn't a fit behind—eat the fruit and spit out the seeds, as they say. It's all one big outlet store where we're digging through racks of clothing looking for outfits that fit the current trends, our needs, and mood. Don't get too attached either! You will be throwing some of that stuff out once it's served its purpose. That's just how it works. You're evolving, and your beliefs will as well.

SOUL ASSIGNMENT:

Can you think of a time when you were mad at yourself because you took someone's advice and you didn't like the outcome?

> *Why didn't you trust yourself?*
> *What were the feelings that showed up when you went*
> *   against your better judgment?*
> *What did this experience teach you?*
> *When situations like this come up again, what will you*
> *   do and how will you give yourself time and space*
> *   to make sure you feel more aligned with the choices*
> *   you'll be making?*

TRIBE DISCUSSION:

Start out each discussion by sharing what you're grateful for, excited about, and your answers for the questions above. Then, complete the statement below. Remember to respect time and adhere to tribe agreements.

> *Something else that came up for me during this exercise was . . .*

REMINDER:

Don't forget to set the appointment for your next tribe meeting and choose what chapter or chapters you will discuss next. (Suggestion: Continue on to read chapter 8 on your own and complete the Soul Assignment, but wait to do the Tribe Work together during your next meeting.)

eight

AGREEMENT 2: RELEASE EXPECTATIONS

We've all got 'em, and they're making us miserable. We have expectations for ourselves, our friends, our spouses, our income, our families, all of it! Don't think so? Ask yourself when was the last time you were disappointed and what was it about. Was it because you had a different vision of how someone should have acted or how that event or situation should have gone and it didn't match? Thought so. My friend Christine Hassler fittingly calls this an "Expectation Hangover," which is also what she titled her book.

My husband and I joke about creating a reality show to rival *The Bachelor* and see if we couldn't actually have a successful match-making track record. It would be called *Don't Get Your Hopes Up*. Each contestant would be given a long list of not-so-flattering details on the eligible person and would be told to lower their expectations. After first getting hit with disappointment, then they go on dates with directions to "Focus on what is good about them and allow yourself to be surprised!" But instead of lavish dates to exotic places with cocktail attire and full hair and makeup, they would be going on dates in their "comfies" to the grocery store, the gym, doing yard work, making dinner together, and babysitting. That way they are completely free of expectation and, in fact, they get to be surprised by the fact that maybe the person is not a total D-bag and perhaps they are a grocery-shopping, lawn-mowing, diaper-changing ninja—someone you could really see yourself wanting to hunker down in a cave with till you die. Our show may actually have a successful track record of keeping couples together because of the lack of expectations and pressure.

In terms of my own high expectations for my girlfriends, *Anne of Green Gables* destroyed me. It was one of my favorite movies (the 1985 miniseries based off the novel written in 1908), about the adventures of Anne Shirley, an eleven-year-old orphan girl who is mistakenly sent to Matthew and Marilla Cuthbert, a middle-aged brother and sister who had intended to adopt a boy to help them on their farm. Instead they got Anne, a boisterous, free soul who was wild, funny, and far ahead of her time. Anne basically set an expectation that I would find my ride-or-die-bestie, my Diana Barry, and through heartbreak, wedding, and babies we would have each other's backs.

The problem was, I found many Dianas, but eventually they would always break my heart or disappoint me. I couldn't find that one best friend who could fulfill everything, like the bosom friend that Anne had. There's a quote from the book that I fell in love with.

There's such a lot of different Annes in me. I sometimes think that is why I'm such a troublesome person. If I was just the one Anne it would be ever so much more comfortable, but then it wouldn't be half so interesting.

—ANNE SHIRLEY

This is where any relationship can get complicated. Everyone has multiple versions of themselves, which also means we have multiple needs and desires, but we tend to give those up to fit an expectation others have for us or we want others to give themselves up to fit ours.

It's when we EXPECT other people to be everything for us or only be the person that we thought we met at first who we "really hit it off with" that we start to feel like a "troublesome person" with troublesome relationships.

Here's a great example of why so many of us either never go on a "second date" or have our expectations crushed. We tend to put our best foot forward when meeting people. We then hold ourselves to show up as that person, while also holding others to that same standard as well. The truth is, this is way too tiring, challenging, the pressure is out of control—not to mention how constricting our "nice" clothes are. This is where we either decide to call it quits because we are too exhausted to keep turning it on, or we eventually get let down by them or worse, we let them down.

No one can or will ever be everything we "need" them to be as long as we are *needing* them to be something to us. First off, if we expect someone to complete us, we have some self-love work to do or we will continue to only look at others as compensation on a debt they can't pay. But before we go there, let's first work on our expectations so we can free others and ourselves.

When we hold expectations of others, we don't allow them to show up in the way they are meant. It's like you're the casting director of your life—telling people where they fit, how to be, and what gap and role they need to fill to make your film go as you want. Essentially, by trying to control how you want things to go, you miss the gifts you're intended to receive and the roles they are actually meant to fill in your life. In our lives we will have a few interchangeable main characters and many, many, many that make up our supporting cast. Your supporting cast is just as important as the main characters because the supporting cast allows the main characters to not have to be everything for you! I'll say this a lot, but release others by "collecting people." Find the role they play best, let them play it, and find someone else for the other roles you desire for your life.

Be aware that expectations can pop up in many different forms when you're trying to connect to your like-minded tribe. Here's one common scenario:

You meet an amazing woman at a party and you totally hit it off! You ask her to get together because you seem to share common interests. The next time you see her she seems different (or maybe you have done this!). Or she just disappears altogether and doesn't respond to your emails or texts—"What a flake." Oops—that's what I catch myself saying before I choose a more empowering thought.

What's most likely going on:

» *She doesn't have the energy to show up as the person she thinks you expect her to be.*
» *She fears you may expect more time and effort out of her than she has to give.*
» *She has a hard time with boundaries and struggles with wanting everyone to like her.*
» *She says yes to everything and later realizes she has no time or energy, but instead of confronting you with honesty, she avoids you to avoid pain.*
» *There was not as strong of a connection on her end but she doesn't know how to say no or not hurt your feelings.*
» *There were no agreements made or boundaries agreed to, so it all just seems too scary to enter into a possibly exhausting, time-consuming relationship like those she's had in the past with women.*

Your expectation: to start creating a relationship with her based off your initial meeting. When that didn't happen, you most likely felt disappointed, hurt, or you took it personal.

Her expectation: She most likely projected a past expectation on herself of how she thought she needed to be or of a past experience of friendships that left her disappointed, exhausted, or hurt.

Either way, you can see how these expectations and lack of communication can take over and we choose to go back to past beliefs that we put on ourselves and others before we even give the relationship the opportunity to happen.

FREE YOURSELF

If having an honest conversation stating your intentions or setting guidelines on what you are looking for (example—a workout once a month with a thirty-minute coffee date after to chat about xyz) doesn't clear the air and make her feel safe to enter into this relationship, then you must release your expectation of whatever it is you wanted. The important part is that after feeling your initial disappointment, you release it without being resentful or pissed (refer to "Don't Take It Personal" on page 118). We are all just doing the best we can. Understand that she is in her own battle with managing her fears, desire to be loved, schedule, and boundaries. Free yourself and her by energetically letting go of the thoughts tied to the experience and mentally sending her love. Your job is to just say "All good! NEXT!" I will give you specific tools on this at the end of this chapter.

> *He who trims himself to suit everyone will soon whittle himself away.*
>
> —RAYMOND HULL

There is this point where once you start living as who you really are, it feels so good and so absolutely affirmative that you just can't go back to censoring yourself to make others happy, even if you know this might make them unhappy and the opinions are coming for you. You've grown too big for the old box and it just doesn't fit anymore, no matter how much you try to grease yourself up, you ain't gonna squeeze back in.

I recently caught myself trying to fit back into an old box. The box was titled "*What people expect from me.*" And below that it read, "Be nice even if people are rude, dress modestly, avoid swearing, sharing your success or true feelings on spirituality, and never ever do anything that makes people uncomfortable." This box had returned from the past with a vengeance, and I knew it was because I was ready and being called to step into who I am in an even bigger way.

The more work I did around creating these tribes of women and friends with whom I felt totally free, blissed, connected, and myself with, the bigger the contrast became when I wasn't being myself. The pain of suppressing who I really was began to outweigh the pain of not pleasing everyone. Why? Because before you can make anyone else happy, you have to make yourself happy. I knew in order to free other women, I had to first free myself. This meant learning to make it a practice to check in when I was following my truth or when I was denying my soul the chance to express itself in every situation. I had to release the old expectations I had for myself and free everyone else from mine as well.

Denying myself experiences because of fear is a habit
I'm trying to quit.

I started observing who I was dressing to please, who I was censoring what I would say around, who I was avoiding sharing my truth with, or who I was trying to make like me even though I didn't like myself around them. I started dabbling in wearing what I wanted even if I was worried it was too sexy or edgy for some. I started saying how I felt as long as I had the highest intentions of love and peace. I started taking a loving yet clear stand if someone was continually harming myself or others. I started to realize sometimes allowing no response to something that is not going to go anywhere positive was the best response.

Although this poked the bear a bit and stirred the pot for some, it allowed the people who needed to hear my message to hear it loud and clear, and forced those who were loving me with contingencies or clinging to the inauthentic side of me to leave. They tend to leave in a huff or with some nasty words, but nonetheless, they go—and a clearing is created when they leave. Don't worry though; after the dust and pain settles, the right people finally have the room to come in. This practice of letting it be okay to let people down as long as my choices felt right for me also released me from expectations placed on me. I am proud to shout from the rooftops that I am human AF—not perfect.

Every day I practice letting go of the expectation that I need to meet everyone else's. The more "me" that I can be, the more I understand that freedom comes from acceptance of self-as-is, and acceptance of what is. Every day I practice releasing others, especially the main characters in my life. I now understand that the more "them" they are, the happier and more free they become as well. This only enhances and complements your life, and they typically end up energetically freeing you just by you freeing them.

Here are three steps to help you through the expectation spiral.

Step 1: See it with new lenses. Instead of focusing on your disappointment or what went wrong, try this:

Ask yourself, what is here for me to learn?

How can I accept this outcome and release my expectation?

Step 2: Challenge your beliefs, thoughts, and reality. Ask yourself, whose expectation is this really?

Is this really how I feel or was this an expectation that was put on me or that I put on myself?

Is this an outdated idea or belief that is no longer serving me?

Step 3: Bend. Be flexible. Being rigid doesn't allow any room for others to show up in their authentic truth on your journey. Release them from being what you think you want them to be. Let them play the complementary role they are for you even if it's just to bring contrast for the good stuff.

Remember that some people are meant to be with you through the entire saga of your life, others for one movie, and some just for a brief scene. Appreciate, allow, bend, and for Pete's sake improve the shit out of your life and have some fun. No one wants to only have one genre to choose from. Take a note from Melissa McCarthy—"Nothing's more charming than someone who doesn't take herself too seriously."

Try repeating these quick mantras when you feel the "Expectation Hangover" coming on.

> *Stop expecting and start exploring.*
> *High standards, low expectations, and a fuck ton of love.*
> *Don't expect, ACCEPT.*

*I release you and accept you for the teacher you are in
my life.*

SOUL ASSIGNMENT:

Try thinking of the last time you felt let down by something or
someone and complete the statements below.

> *What I expected was . . .*
> *What I now accept is . . .*

> *I was let down by . . .*
> *What I learned was . . .*

> *From this experience, I expected . . .*
> *Instead I will explore . . .*

> *When situations like this come up again, my new
> response will be . . .*

TRIBE DISCUSSION:

Start out each discussion by sharing what you're grateful for,
excited about, and your answers for the statements above. Then,
complete the statement below. Remember to respect time and
adhere to tribe agreements.

> *Something else that came up for me during this
> exercise was . . .*

REMINDER:

Don't forget to set the appointment for your next tribe meeting and choose what chapter or chapters you will discuss next. (Suggestion: Continue on to read chapter 9 on your own and complete the Soul Assignment, but wait to do the Tribe Work together during your next meeting.)

nine

AGREEMENT 3: NO GOSSIP

Be impeccable with your word. Speak with Integrity. Say only what you mean. Avoid using the word to speak against yourself or to gossip about others. Use the power of your word in the direction of truth and love.
—DON MIGUEL RUIZ

Even for all of you Superwomen, gossip is kryptonite. Honest, open communication is your sun. You must use your power—your voice—for good at all costs, or it will be the termination of community and relationships in your life.

I recently had to process some gossip I heard about myself. I asked a friend if she would help me release it and find a solution. The gossip was completely made up and the person who said it for sure never thought it would ever get back to me—but boy did it suck when it did. It was said by a woman who has done this to me before, but I forgave her, realizing she had grown and it was in the past. I was struggling with my intuition of letting her back in and getting close to her. Despite my unsure gut feelings, I rekindled our friendship. My friend who was helping me process reminded me of the importance of honoring my anger because I usually try to skip over the pain and shove the emotions down. So with that said, I felt safe to go for it. I was pissed. I was mean. I was swirling so intensely in the eye of the storm that I felt dizzy. I imagined the worst. I had visions that she was going to try to take away everyone I loved and turn them against me—clearly conjuring a deep-rooted fear from being kicked out of tribes (my "why" for this book). I then talked about how uncontrollably angry I felt and how this was making me blind to anything but hatred. I wanted to drag everything bad I've ever known about her out and hurt her like she hurt me. Then I just chanted the F word like it was a prayer that could save me and I imagined everyone "knowing the truth" about who she really is. I felt foolish, betrayed, and deeply hurt. I bawled and yelled and my confusion made me question myself and my choices. I felt like Nancy Kerrigan right after the crowbar.

And then, the next day . . . the anger spit me out. I felt totally hungover and my eyes were still puffy from the tears. I had cried and purged my way to clarity and freedom. I could see the woman who hurt me with compassion because that was the intention and prayer I held from the start. I also had complete clarity around our previously questionable relationship. In the past I would have cut her out and held a grudge. I could now see this was coming from the need to be loved, but I now have a boundary for my safety and she was just not meant to be in my inner circle or the inner workings of my heart.

I know that without these experiences that get our attention, we don't really understand or learn boundaries and forgiveness. I know that nothing can harm me or take away everything and what does happen is a lesson to help me move into the next level of my life and faith. I know she is a mirror and reminder for me. I know that people at their core want to be good. I know that holding on to the anger and hate blocks my blessings.

This and the MANY other like experiences I've had always shake me for a second. They make me want to guard my heart, go back to building my wall, and question if it's even worth it. I found it so perfect that this happened the week before embarking on dissecting this chapter. I felt pretty removed from gossip up to this point, so I was having trouble writing about the feelings around it, and because I choose the belief that everything is always working in our favor, I can see this as a gift to relate and offer up the tools I'm using. I didn't have these tools years ago to see it this way, so these were the exact experiences that would drag on for months if not years and make me go back to isolation.

So here is where I want to help you differentiate between the good, the necessary, and the harmful types of gossip.

I have been on both sides. I've feasted on gossip and I've been the feast. Speaking from experience, they are both detrimental. Gossip is the fast food of conversation—it's easy, cheap, makes you feel like garbage when you're done, and it leaves you craving more junk. It's an ugly addiction with harmful side effects for everyone involved.

Passively listening to gossip or negative talk is an implied agreement.

—SCOTT HARDY

If you are allowing it in your presence and not stopping, disengaging, or standing up for it, you're still going to feel like the greasy side of fries in that not-so-happy meal—but don't worry! We will give you the tools to abolish the mean-girl talk in a nice-girl way.

But first I gotta go deep here because what we're really dealing with is the grown-girl version of bullying. Gossip is a karmic boomerang because words are energy. Words hold the energy of love or fear. They heal or cut. They are life or death. We love with words, fight with words, and people choose to create or end their lives because of words. Words hit harder and hurt longer than actual physically inflicted pain.

We've all been hurt by it and have hurt someone. We may not have meant to harm or even known it got back to them, but it is landing somewhere and leaving an energetic dent. What goes up, must come down. What you say will come back—make sure you're throwing roses, not daggers.

Gossip can take many forms. The mothership is called MALICIOUS gossip. I define this as the premeditated murder of another person's soul through your words. I'm being dramatic because you must know that when you gossip about people with the intention of causing harm, swaying opinions, and tainting their reputation, you could be forever creating a ripple in their lives that you can't undo. You are potentially destroying or harming their lives based on one-sided or false evidence. You don't ever have all the details or know what's going on for people, and even if you did, this will only bite you in the butt and lead you into living in the painful world you were trying to inflict on them.

Gossip says more to me about you than it does about them.

Gossip is the language of small minds. Research shows people who gossip have high levels of anxiety. This is no surprise to me . . . The backlash from gossip is guilt and fear. You never know if your false or malicious secret is safe. Gossipers usually don't have close friends because they can't be trusted, or the friends they have take turns throwing each other under the bus. The gossiper's perspective of the world is that they are being judged and talked about by others. This is because they live in the world they create. They use gossip as their defense and attack. They are as equally obsessed as they are anxiety-ridden and miserable because of their addiction.

How we be is all we see.

Reasons we gossip:

Boredom
Justifying
Jealousy
Fitting in
Misery

Feeling threatened
Insecurity
Retaliation

We want to be viewed as powerful as we know we are, but we are giving our power away every time we gossip, judge, backstab, and undermine each other. We degrade and gossip over our sexual orientation, bodies, jobs, education, political views, religious beliefs, skin color, hair color, how we raise our children, and more. THIS HAS TO STOP or the cycle will get worse. You are either a part of the solution or a part of the problem. We hold the power. Our daughters and the future of the world are begging you. Choose now.

Gossip dies when it hits the ears of the wise.

—UNKNOWN

BE A GOSSIP KILLER

There is a difference between malicious gossip, processing, and blowing off steam, and it's important to differentiate between them. You can't avoid the need to discuss and process events, people, or things that have occurred in your life, especially when they rock your world, because "Feelings buried alive never die," as Karol K. Truman talks about in her book. It's also important to feel and work through the pain caused when you have been the victim or when you realize you may be feeding into rumors, fear, and negative conversations so they don't manifest later in some other way in our bodies and lives.

The good kind of gossip will be driven by the purpose of seeking a solution, peace, and forgiveness. It will be discussed with a single person or trusted group that you know is also committed to the peaceful solution and will not allow any of the words from either party to sway their opinions, but instead they will hold space for the healing and highest good of all involved. They will know that the details, lives, and feelings call for the deepest compassion and they are simply there to help move through to the other side and process the emotion. The details and conversation will never move past this sacred space that is being held.

Here's the good kind of gossip:

"Hey, I heard Angela is having a hard time in her family right now. Let's reach out and see if there is something we can do to help her."

Here's the necessary kind of gossip:

"I was wondering if you could hold some space for me to talk through a situation I had with someone. I'm really upset and I need to just say everything I feel without swaying your opinion, and I'm wondering if you could help me through it and find a solution and a way to forgive this person?"

Here's the malicious kind of gossip to avoid at all costs:

"Did you hear about Nancy? I heard her marriage is struggling. She also went on a trip and I saw a picture of her with some guy on her Instagram. You know, her husband always seemed naïve; I bet she's cheating on him."

Great minds discuss ideas; average minds discuss events; small minds discuss people.

—ELEANOR ROOSEVELT

Look, gossip is going to happen and I wish I could protect you from it, but at the end of the day, you need it. Yup, I said need.

Nothing makes you stand up for what you believe faster than the doubters.

Nothing makes you more clear on your path than the judgment.

Nothing makes you stronger than having to BE your beliefs when they are challenged.

Nothing makes you more compassionate than pain.

Nothing makes you understand forgiveness like hurt.

If you asked for strength and understanding like I did, you may have been given the gossip and judgment as a way for you to get stronger, have more compassion, and understand the underlying reasons humans do certain things.

Lasting pain comes from thinking we shouldn't have to experience any. When we ask for something, we will always be provided with the way in which to get it.

Rule of thumb: Nothing gets spoken until you put it through the Gossip Gauntlet!

Here are some steps for dealing with gossip:

When finding yourself talking about others, ask:

» *Is this gossip good, necessary, or malicious?*
» *How does it make you feel?*
» *What is your intention behind talking about this person?*
» *Does this topic affect you or are you using it for entertainment?*

When you have been the victim of gossip:
Take a breath . . . I see you, I feel you, and I'm sorry you ex-perienced this. You're not alone and God knows the truth. You must have faith in knowing you will be protected. There is an irreplaceable lesson of love, forgiveness, boundaries, and some-thing beautiful on the other side for you.

» *Find a safe person or select few people (as few as possible) to release your feelings with.*
» *Set the intention of finding a solution.*
» *Ask yourself if confronting the person would be the best solution or add to the problem.*
» *Pray for guidance on an answer and to forgive and move forward.*
» *Look for the lesson once you have moved through and released the feelings.*
» *Have faith knowing that how you're able to BE will always win over what people say.*
» *Give it time and know that it will pass and the truth will always come through.*
» *Trust that the people who matter won't listen and it will just reflect on the person speaking it. Remember that "gossip dies when it hits the ears of the wise."*

When you have spread malicious gossip:

First, we've all done it and it doesn't make you terrible as long as you are now aware. You can breathe easy knowing you are still loved.

» *Go to the person and tell them what you said and ask to be forgiven.*
» *Talk to every single person you told and tell them that you were in the wrong.*
» *Even if you think they deserved it or it's "true" (I say that loosely), go to all parties involved and let them know you don't know the situation and that you do not want what you said to sway their opinion and you would like to apologize for involving them.*

When you are caught in the middle or keep finding yourself surrounded by gossip:

Whether you feel like you'll get kicked out of the club or made fun of, standing up for the person, squashing it, or changing the subject will always be actions that will bless your life, clear your conscience, and determine what you are attracting.

It's not easy to do this, but the chain reaction and payoff of spreading love is the difference between a chaotic life or an epic one.

» *Shut it down. Say something like, "I'm on a gossip detox right now, I've been caught in the middle before so I'm trying to quit."*
» *Change the subject.*

» *If it persists, let them know you don't want any part of the conversation.*
» *Leave. Walk away. RUN. Do anything to get that low-vibe bullshit away from your high-vibey self. Even if it means they think you're a weirdo. Be the light.*

Create a ZERO-TOLERANCE rule for gossip in your household, workplace, and in your life. Make sure if you talk about people it's to find solutions or celebrate their awesomeness. Watch your life and relationships become miraculous.

SOUL ASSIGNMENT:

Is there a gossip situation in your life where you would like to make peace?

> *What is it and what solution will you choose?*
> *When situations like this come up again, my new*
>   *response will be . . .*

TRIBE DISCUSSION:

Start out each discussion by sharing what you're grateful for, excited about, and your answers for the statements above. Then, complete the statement below. Remember to respect time and adhere to tribe agreements.

> *Something else that came up for me was . . .*

REMINDER:

Don't forget to set the appointment for your next tribe meeting and choose what chapter or chapters you will discuss next. (Suggestion: Continue on to read chapter 10 on your own and complete the Soul Assignment, but wait to do the Tribe Work together during your next meeting.)

ten

AGREEMENT 4: DON'T TAKE IT PERSONAL

Care about what other people think and you will always be their prisoner.

—LAO TZU

This conversation is so important to have right after the topic of gossip, because these two are often found holding hands, skipping circles around you singing na-na-na-boo-boo, taunting you like a couple of little assholes.

Not taking things personal is quite possibly the most challenging practice in the world. At least to me it is. As humans, we are programmed to care about what others think, and most little girls were raised to be people pleasers, so not taking things personally is completely counterintuitive. This is also why amazing women tend to give up their power and shrink, because in order to NOT take things personal, you must care LESS by learning how to "give zero fucks"—as the kids say. Giving ZFs would then, by your "nice girl" standard, mark you as a bad girl. It's not that you won't care about anything, but to move forward and have peace you will have to grasp how to care a lot about very little. This next phrase totally goes against what I believe, but I think you'll feel me when I say "the struggle is real."

You must care less, in order to care more.

We need more good women to care less. This is not to be confused with being careless, complacent, or naive. When you care too much about what others think, you have nothing left for anything or anyone. Quite honestly, your caring too much is making you do nothing about the things that desperately need doing. Over-caring makes us upset, stressed, and worried, which then leads to exhaustion, confusion, helplessness, and ultimately leaves us feeling paralyzed.

I don't know about you, but I haven't met too many worry-warts who are fulfilled, happy, or making an impact. Letting go, being your authentic self, following your desires despite what people think, and then taking action anyway wipes out worry and anxiety.

It's not about the quantity of people cared about, but the quality of caring.

Stop caring about what people will think if you don't care as much as they think you should! Care MORE about WAY less things! In fact, care about so few things it shocks you and everyone else. This will result in more space to expand your mental capacity to have peace, make REAL change, and be happy. Caring about what others think is actually stopping you from doing what you are here to do—sharing love.

PICK YOUR BATTLES

What will and won't you take personal? Whose opinions will you allow to matter to you? Maybe it doesn't feel like you're allowing people's opinions to hurt you, but choosing to keep thinking about them is, in fact, making the choice to continue the suffering.

> *Pain is inevitable, suffering is optional.*
>
> —UNKNOWN

I can't tell you how many people tell me that fear keeps them from going for their dream, goal, or simply doing more things they love. When we unearth their trepidations, their roots are always wrapped with the terror of what other people will think or say. The most common things I hear are:

"If I start doing things for me or chasing my dreams, my family will think I'm unrealistic and selfish. I can't handle the judgment of them thinking I'll fail or I'm a bad person."

"If I make that decision, no one will support me and people will think I'm crazy or a loser."

"I can't put myself out there because I'm afraid people will criticize or call me a fraud."

Ask yourself this:

> *Are these things true?*
> *What are my intentions?*
> *Is it worth doing even if I fail?*

Will doing what you want make you:

> *A better person? How?*
> *A happier person? How?*
> *A more fulfilled person? How?*

"I'm afraid people will think I am a bad person or just want their money if I advertise my business or charge what I want."

Ask yourself this:

> *Will making money by providing value through my*
> *   services:*
> *Help me provide for myself and my family?*
> *Help others solve a problem or live a more fulfilling life?*
> *Give me more time to spend with my family?*
> *Allow me to have more experiences?*
> *Allow me to free myself from struggle so I can then help*
> *   others?*

You either choose to learn to let go of what people will think in order to fulfill your God-given desires and dreams, or you choose long-term suffering and being held captive by small minds.

People talk. It's a fact of life. I want you to observe for a moment all of the things you have said in your mind about all of the people that you love. Think of all of the nice thoughts and statements and the not-so-nice thoughts and statements. Some people are just wired to state their opinions, and others get their significance by giving unsolicited advice. We say things we don't mean. We vent. We create stories. We make stuff up to feel better and to protect ourselves. We do hurtful, stupid, thoughtless things. We get so caught up in our small worlds that we forget we are coexisting.

Don't take any of it personal. Odds are they aren't giving it the time of day and they probably didn't really mean it. It's your choice if having an honest conversation with the intention of peace is worth having, or if you think this will just add more fuel to the fire—in which case, pick your battles. This is where I let go, set a fierce boundary of where they are allowed in my life, if at all, and send them love. As soon as I calm down, I remember that if they are not fortunate enough to have these tools, then the easy way to feel good is to take cheap shots. Forgive them, let go, choose a new thought, and be that badass, powerhouse goddess who you know you were put on this earth to be. You are here to be the light FOR THEM and the only way to do this is how you BE in these situations.

So what are you going to let matter?

× × ×

Inner peace comes from mastering your mindset.

I have a lot of work floating out there in the world, all of it imperfect. But I'm not willing to live a small, sad life because of small people's opinions of my creativity. I get it, it can be scary out there. It took me one minute and reading five comments under the comments section of my TEDx Talk before I felt like barfing, tapping out of life, and into the lead of *Cast Away: The Sequel*. It's not super fun to pour your entire soul into something only to have people write comments about you looking like a man with plastic boobs and no brain . . . I then remembered what Brené Brown said about criticism after her TED Talk:

> *I carry a small sheet of paper in my wallet that has written on it the names of people whose opinions of me matter. To be on that list, you have to love me for my strengths and struggles.*
>
> —BRENÉ BROWN

Write your list. Stick to it. Check in with it often.

x x x

You will never make everyone happy.

We are so focused on what we think will go wrong instead of what will go right.

Often, it is our own voice that is causing pain and doubt.

Later in the book we will learn to replace it with loving affirmations and faith.

> *People will love you, people will hate you, and none of it will have anything to do with you.*
>
> —ABRAHAM HICKS

In the words of Carly Simon, "You're so vain, you probably think this song is about you." It's NOT about you and it never is. It's about them. No one cares. Don't be such a narcissist and make every passive-aggressive post, comment, or thing about you. At the end of the day, you have to just do what you want because you know if you don't, you'll have destroyed the most important part of your soul and declined the gifts your Creator gave you.

> *But if you do not take it personally, you are immune in the middle of hell. Immunity in the middle of hell is the gift of this agreement.*
>
> —DON MIGUEL RUIZ

HOW TO NOT TAKE IT PERSONAL

Remember that:

> *You don't know what's making them do what they are doing.*
> *They are in pain. Hurt people hurt people.*

They could be trying to protect you in their mind.
What's right for them is not right for you.
They are basing their opinions off their failures,
*   experiences, or fears.*
It's up to you whose opinion actually matters.
No one really cares about anything but what people
*   think of them.*

Accept that you are going to disappoint people.
Focus on your value.
Keep doing things that scare you.
Focus only on what good will come out of it.
Get excited about the growth potential.
Know that whatever and whoever is for you will bring
*   out the best in you.*
Release the rest and thank them for the lessons they
*   provide.*

SOUL ASSIGNMENT:

What is something you've held off on doing because you
*   fear you will be judged for it?*
How are you going to let go and work through the
*   feelings of judgment of others and move forward on*
*   this action?*
What is something you are taking personal and is taking
*   all of your energy away?*

In order to work at not taking this personal I will . . .

TRIBE DISCUSSION:

Start out each discussion by sharing what you're grateful for, excited about, and your answers for the questions above. Then, complete the statement below. Remember to respect time and adhere to tribe agreements.

Something else that came up for me was . . .

REMINDER:

Don't forget to set the appointment for your next tribe meeting and choose what chapter or chapters you will discuss next. (Suggestion: Continue on to read chapter 11 on your own and complete the Soul Assignment, but wait to do the Tribe Work together during your next meeting.)

eleven

AGREEMENT 5: FIERCE BOUNDARIES

"Boundary" by definition is: a line that marks the limits of an area, a dividing line.

Personal boundaries are the lines between your life and personality and those of others. Without them, you will become the stronger energies around you, lose all sense of self, and live on their terms.

Boundaries are there to keep you safe, to protect your soul, time, relationships, finances, businesses, and health. They clearly state what you will and won't accept. When your boundaries are not clearly stated or enforced, it's only a matter of time before you run into problems. Your well-being and your ability to have and keep close relationships depends on your proficiency to say no. Saying no is a self-love practice and the gateway to your greatest sense of self. If you have no boundaries, you most likely feel confused about if you're living your life—or someone else's. Being a "Yes Woman" is the quickest path to denying your truth, neglecting your spirit, and suppressing your personality.

While giving of ourselves and our time comes from a place of love, giving too much comes from a place of need and lack. It stems from the desire to be loved by everyone which most all of us want (but know isn't possible) and comes from a place of never feeling like you are enough. Don't sweat it, we've all been there. It's SUPER DUPER tempting to go there because it's so much easier to make people happy by saying yes to their needs than to deal with the disappointment of saying no and feeling selfish. We would rather run ourselves ragged and give up our happiness and dreams than upset them or have them potentially say a negative thing . . . The problem with that is we end up secretly or not so secretly resenting them and living in anger. The craziest most ass-backward part of all of this is, the more you do for people and the less boundaries you have, the more you get taken for granted and people become resentful of you. If you don't respect your time or yourself, they won't either.

× × ×

A resentful person has no boundaries.

Most problems can be avoided with clear communication and enforcement of our boundaries. It's a lack thereof, however, that causes most of our relationship issues. When you don't have boundaries, you have entered into an unspoken agreement with every relationship you have, which states that you're at their mercy.

Some will respect you and others will walk all over you and suck you dry until there is nothing left of you but regret—usually all done without having any ill intent toward you. You and your lack of boundaries are always just so damn reliable that they can't help but take advantage of your niceties, passiveness, and willingness to make their life easier! You will always end up doing what they prefer to do and you will definitely be the first person asked because they know you won't say no or reject them, because nobody likes rejection. There is no one to blame for you being taken advantage of but you. They have no idea that you are acting this way in all areas of your life. They may actually think you don't have a preference or opinion and that you want to help all the time! You're the one saying yes by not clearly communicating your no.

Whatever is on your plate got there because you said yes to it.

—DANIELLE LAPORTE

Be aware of time thieves.

Your relationships and your tribe will never work out long-term if you don't set clear boundaries on what you will and won't tolerate. Let's use the illustration of being respectful of each other's time—within the tribe and life interactions in general. If one or more women continue to go over their time during the group work (because what they're going through feels extremely important, challenging, etc.) even after you remind them and you continue to put up with it, you will be resentful, feel disrespected, and this thing that was meant to complement your life will then turn into something that messes up your plans and stresses you out. This often happens when women in our lives monopolize the conversation, or won't get off the phone. We feel unimportant, unheard, and used. Although they may not mean it, it sends a message that what they have to say is more important than what you do. These people are called time thieves. Most of them don't even know it—they most likely had to fight for time growing up or they just have the "gift of gab," so remember, an inch in *gab* for them is a mile of annoyance to the more quiet types. You must be aware of them and communicate clearly with how you feel and exactly what you need to continue the relationship, or often they won't get the message. It's up to you to set a boundary and bring it to their attention. If it continues after you've enforced it in a loving way, I'll help you with what to say to them later.

× × ×

Boundaries make room for your blessings.

Creating boundaries feels empowering. Every time you use and enforce them, you have a little more space and you feel a little bit more like yourself, and when you feel like yourself and have a clearing, this sends a message to the universe that you're ready for more of your path to be revealed. Until then you're sending the signal that you won't do what it takes to protect and make room for the blessings that come your way. When you allow yourself to be taken for granted, you are taking the gift from your Creator for granted. Protect it with your life by protecting your desires with your boundaries.

While setting boundaries feels challenging, it also feels so damn delectable to enter into agreements and relationships when you feel clarity and mutual respect around them (this is how relationships are meant to feel!). This gives everyone involved permission to show up as themselves. It takes away the guessing games and passive-aggressive comments that begin to brew when "nice" people avoid confrontation and communication over what each party needs to remain happy in the relationship. Sticking to your boundaries is the hard part. It's the "nice" people with no boundaries who are secret, raging, lonely, passive-aggressive time bombs. I know this because I used to be one. I might have been agreeing to your terms and saying yes with a smile, but my internal dialogue was cussing you out to next Tuesday. Boundaries actually made me less of a secret a-hole.

Now that you've set these boundaries, don't assume that others will stick to them. That expectation will just leave you angry and resentful. Let go of any disappointing expectations and take control by being the enforcer.

Don't fool yourself. If you don't enforce them, you are not in the driver's seat of your life. Boundaries are best when set at the beginning, but you can set them at any time. There will be things that come up along the way that don't quite sit right with you or that feel like a red flag and require a conversation to clear some blurred lines. Squash this mucky area immediately with a conversation and boundary.

When I was dating my husband, he was asked to be in one of his friends' weddings. As a member of the wedding party, it was his responsibility to also go to the bachelor party—and this one was going to include strippers. I learned from my previous relationships that this was a huge jealousy trigger for me, and as much as I wanted to be the cool girlfriend and say, "No problem! Go have a good time!" I just knew I would secretly feel insecure and resent him for going. Because I really respected our relationship and wanted it to work, which meant I had to feel good as well, I asked to have a conversation. While I was afraid of this conversation, I also knew that I needed to be honest and true to who I was, even if that meant he thought I was acting jealous. I needed to make my feelings crystal clear so I didn't become quiet and resentful and he wouldn't misinterpret the unspoken expectations I would put on him.

So we had a talk and I told him how I felt, and you know what: It turned out that my openness gave him permission to share his insecurities as well. We told each other about what triggers us and we agreed to do the best we could and talk about it as things came up. To this day, I have never felt or been told I made him jealous, because we have very clear boundaries. Sixteen years later, we are still creating boundaries in our marriage as things arise. Boundaries help you know who your people are.

Why haven't you created them yet?

It's that word again. FEAR. Along with these fantastic accompaniments:

Losing friends
Losing love

Losing your partner or spouse
Losing your job
No longer feeling important
Being misunderstood
Guilt

You're afraid to lose the things that you're unhappy with because they are familiar. The thing about happiness is that it needs room and lots of it.

Boundaries—not just for bitches

You don't have anxiety because someone or something is stressing you out, you have anxiety because you have no boundaries. We have anxiety over the things we have no boundaries around. Look, I know you're afraid to look like a bitch and have a fear of losing acceptance if you actually enforce them, but every boundary you set makes room for your bliss and frees another woman to set her own boundaries, which frees her self. Bliss takes up space, and if there is no room because you are so full with someone else's agenda, it will never enter. Those who can't respect your boundaries don't yet respect themselves or have any of their own. Have reasonable boundaries. Bend and sway in the wind like a palm tree, but snap back and stand tall when you need to. I'm not saying cut everyone and everything out of your life. I'm saying create lines so your life and relationships work better. Be reasonable, compromise, and if people are continually crossing the line, you gotta get Khaleesi on their asses, call in the dragons (*Game of Thrones*, anyone?), and lay down some fierce ground rules—with love, of course. This isn't about being a cold-hearted bitch. You're doing this because you love yourself, and you want to have a resentment-free relationship with them—I know I would prefer that over someone secretly feeling annoyed with me any day. Be open, be accessible, but respect yourself and your gifts by having shop hours and a door with a lock when you need it.

× × ×

Here are some things to remember about saying NO:

You're the one saying yes to the stress, by not saying no.

When you say no to something, you are making room for your yes.

"No" is a complete sentence. Never, ever apologize afterward, this gives them space to convince you and it says to yourself that you should feel bad about your decision. Keep your power by saying "No, but thank you for thinking of me" instead.

Saying no is a self-love practice. Saying no protects your physical and mental health.

× × ×

Tips to measure if something is or isn't for you:

"If it's not a hell yes, it's a hell no." I've heard this many times from so many huge mentors in my life and I've adopted it. If it's not something that gets me excited, it's simply not meant for me and it's a distraction. Not all good things are good for you, and if it doesn't give you energy or align with your one- to five-year vision, then it's a NO.

Very successful people say no to almost everything.

—WARREN BUFFET

I'm actually as proud of the things we haven't done as the things I have done.

—STEVE JOBS

Steve Jobs also shared that focus is not about the thing itself but about saying no to all of the other good ideas. Again, boundaries.

× × ×

Scripts for setting boundaries and saying no in some of the most common areas:

I share scripts because when I started in sales I needed to learn a new form of communication. Because I had zero experience, I researched scripts that worked for others which I could read off until I found my own authentic style and voice. The scripts felt like I had someone holding my hand reminding me I had backup until I felt comfortable. This worked wonders for my sales career and proved to work its magic for all my tough conversations as well.

For time thieves, try this:

"I love our chats and I'm wondering if you could help me with something. In most of my relationships I find that I tend to choose to take the role of listener, and because I don't speak up I end up feeling like I don't have a place to share what's going on in my life. I would love if you would make sure that I share equally in our conversations and remind me to share what's been going on with me. Will you help me with this?"

"I would love to chat with you about something weighing on my heart because I care about our relationship, if you're open. You are an amazing person and I value our friendship, so I just wanted to say that sometimes I feel less important or not heard when my time is (not respected or overlooked). I know it's not intentional, but I never want to feel resentful for something that could be taken care of with a simple conversation. Thank you so much for letting me share that with you, and I hope you share your feelings with me."

For romantic relationships:

"I have to share my feelings with you about something with the intentions of always being open in order to grow together and because I always want to be honest and work through anything that could create an issue down the road.

Do I have your permission to share openly? I care deeply about you, and that's why I want to tell you that . . . (here is where you would say with love how you have been feeling and state a request, or a request with a conversation to compromise)."

× × ×

Tips and scripts for saying NO:

Simply say, "No, thank you. Have a great day!"

Look, if you know you're not going to go to something or do something, stop saying "maybe" or "let me get back to you." All you're doing is stringing their hopes along and postponing your no, wasting energy and making it even more painful later. There is nothing worse than someone who tells you what you want to hear to your face but never follows through. People will have so much more respect for you if you stop wasting their time and just be honest with them. "Eat that frog," do the tough stuff as it arises, free yourself immediately, and try this instead:

"Thank you so much for considering me. I won't be able to participate/help out at this time. I'm honored to have been asked."

"I am unable to make it to this event, but thank you so much for the invite and I'm sending all my well wishes for a lovely time had by all!"

"Thank you for the continued invites and I just want to be up-front and let you know that I am trying to remove things from my plate right now so I can have more time for my relationships and some projects (or yourself or personal health or whatever!), but I am so grateful that you thought of me. Thank you. Feel free to circle back in a couple months (or don't write that if you don't mean it!).

The firm no:

"No, thank you, and thank you for respecting my final decision."

SOUL ASSIGNMENT:

> *What is the most pressing boundary you need to set right now? For example, schedule, saying no, etc.*
> *How will you do it (or say it)?*
> *What will you gain by setting this boundary?*
> *What are you willing to lose because of what you will gain?*
> *When situations like this come up again, my new response will be . . .*

TRIBE DISCUSSION:

Start out each discussion by sharing what you're grateful for, excited about, and your answers for the questions above. Then, complete the statement below. Remember to respect time and adhere to tribe agreements.

Something else that came up for me was . . .

REMINDER:

Don't forget to set the appointment for your next tribe meeting and choose what chapter or chapters you will discuss next. (Suggestion: Continue on to read chapter 12 on your own and complete the Soul Assignment, but wait to do the Tribe Work together during your next meeting.)

twelve

AGREEMENT 6: BE AUTHENTIC

To be you feels like truth. To live your truth feels like bliss. Being the authentic you is bliss.

Choosing to be authentic is the path to following your bliss. Put simply, it means, "Be happier by being more 'you.'" Easy, right? Ha! You might be saying, "Thanks, genius! If I knew how to be happy, I wouldn't need this book." Before we jump into what authenticity is, I want to let you know that in section 3 of this book you will be doing a deep dive into who you are and figuring out what makes you tick, but for now let's talk about what role authenticity plays in your bliss. I kinda feel like it's one of those topics that you have to get lost in before you can be found—meaning when you ask yourself questions to try to find your authentic self, it can often lead to multiple layers of even deeper questions before you find what feels like truth for you. Just go with it and see what joy you can find in the unraveling.

While researching this topic, I loved what author and psychologist Nina Burrowes had to say on it:

If you want to understand the true meaning of authenticity you need to go back to its root. The Latin root of the word "authenticity" is "author," so being "authentic" doesn't mean being honest about who you are, it's about being your own "author." Authenticity is an active and creative process. It's not about revealing something, it's about building something; and that something is "you."

In today's world, we're inundated with social media, ads, and fake-reality everything . . . we are starved for authenticity. This constant exposure has made us awfully good at sniffing out what does and doesn't feel authentic to us. And while we are seeing more and more efforts around this, we're also being manipulated by the idea that we have to spill our guts to be considered "real," and that can be even scarier than being seen as fake. Calm down, heavy breather, before you go putting live webcams in every part of your house, this does not mean you have to "expose" yourself to the world for your business to work, or tell everyone about that time you peed your pants when you were twelve on the bus and blamed your seat mate (unless of course that makes you feel better), to be a better human. You just have to start being, acting, and unapologetically showing up as the you that you are, authoring from here on out.

We are going to practice what it feels like on the small stuff first, so you have a good foundation of confidence and what it feels like to follow your authentic path. I'll share the how-to at the end so let's keep unraveling!

Being authentic is a serious daily practice that never ever ends. I observe myself being inauthentic every single day to avoid conflict, whether it's saying my coffee order is fan-fricken-tastic when it tastes like a cup of burnt hair, or not walking away from a conversation that makes me puke a little bit in my mouth . . . Instead of choosing to speak up nicely or walk away, I choose inner conflict. These are some of the smaller examples I was mentioning that are good starter points on which to practice.

I know I'm not alone because I see and hear it everywhere. Women not wearing what they want to wear, settling for jobs they don't feel are a fit, eating food they don't want to eat, and continuing to spend time with the people who make them feel terrible out of fear of not fitting in. "Are you really gonna eat a salad and make us feel bad about ourselves while we eat burgers? C'mon, just one burger won't kill you." Or "Do you think you'll be taken seriously if you wear that dress and bright lipstick to speak?" Or "If you would have spoken up or shared your ideas we would have promoted you instead." It's the denying of one's talents, skills, truth, and core desires in order to make others feel okay.

There was a point in my life where all the imposter alarms in my body and mind were constantly going off—except they were about me. The alarms came in the form of discomfort in groups, irritation with not feeling like I was able to be myself, and anxiety over fear of sharing things I really wanted to share. I was living in a constant state of disgust—not disgust of others, but with myself. I got so fed up with not being me, doing the things I desired, saying how I felt, sharing my gifts, or offering my valuable opinions and ideas, that I wanted to escape my own fakeness. I would have bouts of angst, crying fits, alcohol binges, and I would find myself numbing out the pain of not following my truth in the most wasteful, time-consuming ways from online shopping to going through my closet for things to donate. I was tired all of the time from following ideas that didn't align with my soul. Exhaustion, restlessness, and boredom are always signs for me that it's time to check in with how I'm showing up and what I'm spending my time doing.

If you're afraid to be yourself in the groups you hang out in now because of being judged, that's a huge sign that you're not hanging with authentic people. This doesn't make them bad, though! This does, however, mean they are afraid to be themselves as well, and that will make it impossible to have a real connection. People who are very judgmental are the ones who are feeling the most judged in their minds. That constant fear makes them choose the safest, most presentable version of themselves. It also makes it hard to create a solid relationship when everyone shows up to the party afraid to be who they really are. The more authentic you are the more they may reject you, because they fear and reject that part of themselves. If this happens it just means they are not ready to see and share their truth and that's okay, it clears space for the people that will celebrate you because your truth invites them to show up free to be themselves. Now that's some *real* feel-good shiz right there.

For some people who are not doing any work around self-awareness, being authentic can often get confused with staying the same. This can then feel inauthentic when people say to us, "You've changed." Or "I miss the old you." This can especially feel gut-wrenching when it's said in a negative way by someone from our past or a family member who "knows us better than anyone else." Changing can be frowned upon by those who love certainty and hate getting uncomfortable. These two things, however, are killers of growth, which is the purpose of life and becoming authenically YOU, which is how you follow your bliss.

Evolving is the lifeblood in the body of bliss. I may lose some of you when I say that some of your family and friends may not be in alignment with your journey. Part of being self-aware is knowing when someone is no longer meant to be walking in front of you or by your side, and when it's okay to pass them. Transcending the old familiar you is one of the hardest things we will ever do because you have to say goodbye to your old life, and sometimes those in it, if they're not willing to support or accept this upgraded version of you. Being true to your calling from your Creator might mean making peace with the idea that some people in your life may never be the version of happy that you have come to understand and know. Being authentic does not mean worrying about bringing others with you, feeling terrible that you have outgrown someone and making their growth and happiness your responsibility; instead it's allowing yourself to be pulled forward in the direction of your soul while the ones you traveled with choose to stay back, making peace with where they're at.

For some people, taking a break for a short amount of time (or permanently) from those holding them down or hurting them is the only way to free themselves and follow their authentic path. This is usually just as painful as it is important, if those people begin to harm your mental or physical health. I had to do this with some family members for a few years (some longer) because I wasn't strong enough to transcend the beliefs and mentality that we were stuck, depressed, couldn't make money or be fit, and that life was hard. My soul kept trying to steer me toward joy, but the more time I would spend around them, the more I felt myself slipping into a dark place.

I knew in order to save myself I had to go. I had to be around new ideas and people who thought differently, until I truly believed these ideas myself, saw them at work, and felt strong enough to be able to spend time with my family years later without getting sucked back in. If your family and old friends are constantly pulling you back to a place that lowers your energy and makes you unhappy, you have to figure out how much time is too much and where the boundaries are for you. I still struggle with this to be totally honest, but the more I accept them for who they are and allow myself to be me as much as possible, the easier it gets.

Observing how you feel around and away from them will start to teach you how much time is healthy and what the things and topics you can do and discuss are in order to keep feelings from heading south. The lowering of your energy to match theirs serves no one, including them. Your happiness and positive outlook, however, inspires and elevates everyone. In time, even the ones who seem to want to pull you back the most tend to come around, because you become the proof that it can be done. The only way to change your family legacy is to break the chain and old patterns. Keep going even when fear comes in and tries to make you feel awful for feeling good and thinking you could have a better life. Eventually the ones who are ready to step into their higher purpose will see what happiness looks like and how to do it from watching you.

There is a cost to not being you.

Being authentic is scary because it means the buck begins and ends with you. There is no handing off the blame when you know you made the decision. The thing is, you have to get it wrong and be inauthentic to figure out what it feels like to be in alignment with your truth. This is going to take massive forgiveness, grace, and space. If you don't give yourself the room and quiet time to listen and observe when you're in and when you're out of alignment, you may actually never know or get the benefits.

For me, being out of alignment can feel like I betrayed myself. This could come after being around people who don't elevate me, doing things that are distracting or low vibe, or not speaking my heart when I know I'm supposed to in order to fit in. When I'm out of alignment, I feel like things are forced, like I need a shower—yucky, like I'm tired and anxious at the same time and like something is wrong or missing.

The dance of authenticity is knowing it won't feel perfect when you're on its path. In the beginning you won't realize you're on it until you go off, and that's your cue to ask how you could get back on. The best way I can describe it quickly is: being authentic feels like freedom and opening; being inauthentic feels like a betrayal and a cutting off. No part of being authentic guarantees people will like you. In fact, it narrows down your search for your like-minded tribe rather quickly and effectively! You're either really going to be for someone—or not. You're no longer bending for them when you don't want to and they may not like who you really are, your views, or whatever!

It's going to take all the grace you have to accept and understand this bliss journey, or this journey to becoming the authentic you. It's sharing who you are even when you're not who you think your mom, I mean people, want you to be. Oftentimes I believe that the only reason we think we have to be a certain way is because we just haven't seen enough examples of other ways of being, getting celebrated, and shared. Have you ever had that moment where a woman shows up in a surprising way that you actually loved and thought, if she can do that, maybe I can too? There are ways to be firm, decisive, and loving; to be you, have boundaries, even in the most challenging of situations—family included. It comes with discomfort, but I live this and it can be done.

You're going to have to embrace feeling vulnerable and dis-liked by some of the people in your life. Being authentic and showing up differently than they expect you to is going to chal-lenge people's beliefs and expectations. They will try to protect themselves from the uncertainty they are feeling around the relationship because change is what causes the most resistance and fear in our lives. The quickest way a person in fear thinks they can gain control back is to manage the other person causing the uncertainty through fear. This new version of you with all of your new perceptions and possibilities may be too much for them, so they will have to do and say hurtful things that make you go back to the old version of you. Your changes threaten their identity and what they believe to be true for themselves. If you are taking action despite your challenges, what does this say about their current choices? This could mean they are not stuck, but they are choosing to stay in their situation. This also means they would have to change and give up their comforts so they react out of fear in order to not have to look at all the pain this brings up.

In order to live in your authentic truth you must be willing to:

Walk alone
Be courageous
Be disruptive and disliked
Be vulnerable
Feel rejected
Take responsibility
Stop judging
Stop complaining
Stop blaming
Consult your inner guide before every decision
Have daily rituals that keep you connected to your truth
Adopt your own definition of authenticity

When you commit to doing this, you tap into your Authentic Power.

While I was at Oprah's SuperSoul Live Session, Gary Zukav, the author of *The Seat of the Soul*, shared how to do this with us. I'll write a quick summary of what he shared:

Every time you choose an intention from love instead of from fear and take action from that place, you tap into your authentic power. The first step to developing emotional awareness around your authentic power is to turn inward instead of acting on an impulse. Give yourself some space and act from the most loving part of your personality. This doesn't mean following every whim, addiction, and desire, it means knowing and staying close to whatever our core desires and values are and having the courage to act totally opposite than you did the day before.

I would also like to add that it's important to have the courage to forgive and immediately try again when you don't do this.

To be authentic means to have experiences that help you move from who you were to who you are becoming. You are always creating the next version of yourself. Every next level of your life will require the next-level version of yourself. Don't resist the upgrade because of the learning curve or lack of understanding from others. When you download better programming, you run faster, smoother, and more efficiently.

Contradict your way to clarity *IF* it feels right—notice I said right and not good? Even truth can have paradoxes. Something can be aligned with your truth but not feel good to know or easy to do initially. Life can hold opposite truths at the exact same time. Don't stay trapped in something simply because it once freed you. You are ever changing. Danielle LaPorte gave me so much clarity and freedom from the dogmatic "black and white" mindset after reading *White Hot Truth* that I created my own list that was true for my life.

Here are some of my paradoxical truths that have personally freed me.

You can both:

> *Keep your agreements and change your mind if you know you MUST.*
> *Change everything including your hair color and love your roots.*

Stand up for your beliefs and sit down and shut up.
Be sexy and feminine and powerfully command respect.
Be spiritual and insanely successful and financially
    abundant.
Be humble and confident AF.
Love freely and protect your heart fiercely.

Confusion is as much a part of authenticity as is courage. Have the courage to create an experience you're confused about to gain more understanding or compassion. Have the courage to be confused on how you feel and to change your mind and stance on something even if it's going to upset people. It's when we feel stuck because we are confused what direction to take that we deny our truth and allow our fear to hold us back from being and doing what we feel called to be or do. Once in a great while commitments and past truths can be broken or reexamined if it means sacrificing your health or stressing for no reason. In this case, have a conversation and negotiate. Most times people will understand but sometimes they won't.

I had a friend who had labeled herself with a specific lifestyle and diet. She was so passionate and got such amazing results that she started a blog and gained a large following. After years of strictly following this regimen, she noticed her health was declining, not because of her lifestyle and diet but because her body was showing to have different needs than the limited options and lack of variety she was choosing. She never imagined she would ever feel differently. She was so scared to tell anyone because of how devout she was to the lifestyle that she felt stuck, scared, and like a horrible fraud. She started adding things to her nutrition that were outside of her former plan and slowly her health improved, but her identity was in crisis. She was constantly feeling out of alignment, and this caused serious turmoil and anxiety. She decided she had to share her truth with her community that she no longer wanted labels on herself and her eating. Although she finally felt free, a tidal wave of hate mail, messages, and death threats came to her. After the tsunami of backlash, she shared that despite it being the most pain and fear she's ever experienced, it was all worth it to have followed her truth in both instances and live in alignment with her soul. She also shared that the choice to follow this lifestyle and diet was at one time in alignment, until it wasn't, and the blessings, wisdom, and happiness she gained afterward far exceeded any of the pain felt. Labels always seem to come with an expiration date.

Here's what it boils down to. When you're in alignment, you're connected to your inner GPS and that GPS changes its locations as we evolve. It will feel like you are getting directions revealed to you one turn at a time to an unknown destination. You'll feel unclear of the path to get there, but certain that where you are being guided is exactly where you want to go. The more you trust that the surprise destination is one that you will love, the more you can sit back and watch as each delightful turn gets revealed to you, one mile at a time. As you continue on this journey, you realize that you're not worried about the final destination because each surprise turn and detour has revealed some unknown area that you love exploring and you may have never seen if you took the direct path to a destination.

Remember, for something new to begin, something old must end—even parts of you that you thought defined you. You are not defined by anyone or anything you did, said, or have, so please STOP apologizing for who you are, how you feel, and everything you do or say. This sends mixed signals to your brain saying it's not safe to be you. Instead of "I'm sorry," try "Pardon me" or "Excuse me, I would like to share something" or "Thank you for holding space and allowing me to express how I feel."

SOUL ASSIGNMENT:

> *Where are you being inauthentic in your life?*
> *What small steps will you take to express your authentic self next time?*

TRIBE DISCUSSION:

Start out each discussion by sharing what you're grateful for, excited about, and your answers for the questions above. Then, complete the statement below. Remember to respect time and adhere to tribe agreements.

> *Something else that came up for me was . . .*

REMINDER:

Don't forget to set the appointment for your next tribe meeting and choose what chapter or chapters you will discuss next. (Suggestion: Continue on to read chapter 13 on your own and complete the Soul Assignment, but wait to do the Tribe Work together during your next meeting.)

thirteen

AGREEMENT 7: "F" YOURSELF AND EVERYONE ELSE

I hope you come down with a serious case of the "F" its. It's complete freedom to "F" yourself and everyone else. Do it in public, do it in private, do it in church. It's hot, sexy, shocking, spiritual, and it makes you feel completely liberated. Did I mention it cranks up your mood, vibe, and manifesting skills faster than any other thing I've tried? Are you in the mood for a good ol' "F" sesh yet?

If you haven't yet figured it out and you're ready to burn this book and save your eyeballs from those graphic mental pictures that you've accidentally enjoyed, the "F" stands for FORGIVE.

That's right, *Forgive Yourself and Everyone Else* every second of every day. And once you're done going down the list, start over at the top and start the "F-ing" all over again.

Wikipedia says forgiveness is the intentional and voluntary process by which a victim undergoes a change in feelings and attitude regarding an offense and lets go of negative emotions, such as vengefulness, with an increased ability to wish the offender well.

But forgiveness isn't done for the sole benefit of your offender. Forgiveness is about transforming the feelings that are causing you pain. Our feelings of pain come from holding on to the anger and pain in the memory. By making the choice to loosen that grip and view the situation from a different perspective (love), we're able to change our thoughts and emotions and free ourselves of this burden. Our thoughts create the world we live in, so when we choose not to forgive, we choose to lock ourselves in a tiny prison cell with our offenders and throw away the key.

A Course in Miracles (*ACIM*) says, "Let me recognize the problem so it can be solved."

This chapter can bring profound healing if you commit to looking at the darkness you may be avoiding with all the compassion and gentleness you can muster up. But please, trust this process and don't stop before you feel even the slightest sense of relief, okay? Keep "F-ing" everyone until you feel better (sorry, I had to bring a little comic relief).

Forgiveness is a choice, a process, and a lifestyle. I live an "F-it" life. It's a way of being that brings complete peace and prevents me from carrying everyone else on my back, which is precisely what we're doing when we don't forgive. "Hop on, hater! I want to give you and all your bullshit a free horsey ride. I'll be down here dying while you enjoy the view."

The most important thing you can know about forgiveness is that you don't need to be ready or understand how to forgive or even what it would look like if you did. You just have to be WILLING to keep trying and asking for help to let go. It's not going to happen overnight, so you can start by forgiving your impatience right now and know that experiencing peace even for one second longer than you did yesterday is progress. You can't get to the other side without going through.

Forgiveness does not make wrong or hurtful things okay—not even close. Forgiveness helps you to loosen and eventually release the grip the person has on you or should we say, the grip you have on the person. This eventually allows you to return back to love, which is where your power and authentic truth lie. Forgiveness lets you off the hook and allows you to stop the continuous replay of the wrongs that occurred.

Forgiving everyone doesn't make you a pushover. In fact, it's quite the opposite, as it puts your power and happiness back into your hands by taking you out of the paralyzing, poisonous thoughts causing you to relive the past in your head. When we're in defense mode, we are thinking of hate, harm, and visualizing a counterattack. Even if this is kept to yourself, you're living the feelings in real time as if it's all happening in the present.

DEFENSIVENESS IS AN OPT-IN

In our defenselessness our safety lies.

—*ACIM*

I love the viewpoint from *ACIM* so, I'm going to paraphrase from the lessons it offers on forgiveness.

By acknowledging our faith and returning to "love," we will

be protected and unharmed. If we doubt this, however, the peace we seek will not be found.

We tend to think that defense is an act of self-preservation, but it's actually a counterattack. Or I like to call it an opt-in. When we feel the need to defend ourselves, we are actually opting to be a part of someone else's illusion. It's like being offended when someone says they don't like your purple hair when you're actually a brunette. You wouldn't need to defend or be hurt because it's not true and it would waste your time and energy and do more harm than good to give it any attention. If you did respond, however, you'd just be giving that illusion fuel, and the person more power, which will grow the negative energy between you. In other words, the more thought and focus you give it, the bigger and more alive it gets.

Defensiveness is a sign that your strength in faith and love is weak and needs attention. By acting defensive, you're saying that you are easily harmed by the false stories of others. You're saying you don't believe you'll be protected if you choose love. Love is how we connect to God, so when we deny its power we are denying our protection from our Creator. We are again buying into human's false perceptions and projections that can harm us.

When you stop defending, the attack seems to disappear over time. We fear that by not responding, we'll get "taken down" or our character will be in jeopardy, but defenselessness doesn't mean you don't do anything. It just means you respond with love instead of an attack. Love is the only power that can diffuse anything. Sometimes the most loving thing you can do is to leave, delete, block, avoid interaction, or not say a word and just allow yourself space to feel, heal, let go, and pray for help to transform your thoughts around the attacks and the attackers.

There will be times when you will have to interact and verbally respond. But there's a way to do this so you can make sure it's a response that frees you rather than one that imprisons you further into their illusion. In this case, be slow to respond so you can give yourself the space to clear the hotness of the anger. When we're angry, hurt, and wounded, we're not thinking or feeling clearly, and it makes attacking back seem like the answer and that it's justified. Breathe and remember that you have no power when you're not coming from love. Even if it feels better in the short term, it won't end well.

There will be times when conversation and massive action need to be taken to remove the person from your life. You may need to let someone know that something was inappropriate and you will no longer allow them to treat you in a certain way or say hurtful things. This is simply a clearing for you to remove them from your life and thoughts and energetically release yourself from their grip. *ACIM* says an attack is a call for love. And when you give yourself time to think and take action from a place of love, you are stripping them of their power and fuel in your life.

APPROACHING SITUATIONS FROM A PLACE OF COMPASSION AND GRATITUDE

Although we are learning how to become quick to forgive, it's not necessarily reconciliation. You can forgive someone but still not trust them to be in your inner tribe again. For instance, I have had some people that I was very close to say and do some gut-wrenching, hurtful things to my husband and me, and after much pain and years of trying to forgive them, I can honestly finally say that I am at peace with everything they put us through. I made the decision to allow them back in my life—but in a different role.

It wasn't the shortest of processes—years to be exact—but the core practices that got me there were compassion and gratitude. Compassion reminded me that their rumors and actions came from a place of insecurity and desire to feel significant. Reminder—don't take it personal! Does this mean we'll be BFFs anytime soon? In some cases that could definitely happen, in this one, not so much, but it does help me appreciate their gifts and approach them with love (albeit from a more aware and protected place). Let's just say, they can come to the White House party, but I'm not letting them in the Oval Office. Oh, and if by chance they pull that same shit again, they will lovingly get escorted out and the gate locks behind them.

Gratitude also proves valuable whenever I get stuck or want to get mad about old feelings or wounds. Without this extreme lesson, I would never have been able to protect myself from more similar (larger) experiences that often come with a very successful business. I know I certainly wouldn't have learned how to create a tribe that is built on solid agreements. I also know that no matter what wound or hurt we are experiencing there is a way through with forgiveness, compassion, and gratitude. Life (shitty experiences included) is all happening for you. There are lessons you need to learn and teach to pass through to the next level of your life. There is much responsibility that comes with our dreams, desires, and evolution, and the only people who can deliver these important lessons are usually the people closest to us. After all, if it was a stranger, it would be a whole lot easier to write off and miss what we needed for the road ahead, right?

How would you understand how to love passionately and forgive freely without being deeply hurt? The answer? You wouldn't. Once the smoke has settled, choose to be grateful for the lesson.

Forgiveness goes hand in hand with surrender.

When life feels out of control and chaotic, when you feel completely misunderstood and maliciously wronged or you don't understand why something is happening . . . surrender it up. Altar it up. Let go and let God. We were created unassailable, and that means we are made of and with God. When you know the problem is not yours to be had and you surrender it over to God, you will start to feel relief. Letting go is an act of faith. When you feel like an out-of-control psycho, it's time to start praying and handing it over. I'll share exactly how to do this at the end of the chapter, but first we're going to go down the list of the most common "bags of sand" that are keeping your hot air balloon from taking flight.

Every time you choose to hold a grudge or keep someone hostage and under watch so they can't hurt you again, you throw another sandbag in your balloon. We're going to go through the list together so we can identify the things you may not even know are keeping you from your freedom.

There's only one thing you need to begin, and that's to just be willing. Take a deep breath right now and say this paraphrased prayer from *A Course in Miracles* out loud with me for every cell and every part of your body and mind that is ready to be free:

"I am willing to forgive. I am willing to see this differently. Please, God, give me the strength to see this differently. I choose to see love instead."

And then I continue to choose a better thought until I feel peace.

"F" Yourself

First off, you must forgive yourself in order to forgive others and free yourself. Did you know one of the biggest things that trips women up on this journey to bliss is the inability to let go of failures? I know this cycle all too well. The guilt, shame, disappointment, pain spiral. *I don't deserve forgiveness, I'm a failure and a terrible person, therefore I will continue to sabotage myself by doing actions that inflict pain, keep me small, and create terrifying horror stories about what people will say and how terribly I will fail if I decide to move forward.*

For starters, let's be gentle with ourselves and remember that Source is only pure love, so much so that we can't wrap our brains around the idea that no matter what we do, we are still loved and forgiven—there are no contingencies on your Creator's love. Choosing the path of love in our darkest hour is truly a warrior's journey. So don't consider even the smallest steps you've taken lightly. When we fail or commit what we feel is a wrong or shameful act, this can feel so shocking and painful that it gets locked into our nervous system, cells, and memory and it is the reference point for everything we do and think moving forward.

We give it power by keeping it hidden in the dark, but also by keeping it at the forefront of our mind. This feeling and memory is what we consult before taking any new action—making the memory part of our identity. To stop this cycle, we're going to deconstruct those stories later, but for now I want you to play with the idea that no matter what you've done or said, you are worthy and you are forgiven. Beating yourself up does not make you a better person, and it certainly doesn't pay for a crime that was already forgiven. Forgiving yourself and coming through the other side, can, however, free you to help others learn how to free themselves from their pain.

Learning from the failure and forgiving yourself is the ultimate payment you can give to God, to yourself, and to everyone around you. To begin, try coming from a place of deep compassion for yourself and seeing yourself through the same eyes as you see a child or someone you love. This will help remind you of what healing and love are waiting for you and how you are doing the best you can in the moment. I often picture God (or whatever you picture as your higher power) taking my face in His hands and gently kissing the top of my head, saying, "You are so loved, child." I can feel Him reminding me that we are His children and He did not create us to be perfect. He expects that mistakes are part of the process, and He reminds me not to miss out on the entire purpose of life—and that is to forgive, give love, heal ourselves so we can help heal others and enjoy this gift of life.

Choose one of the prayers I offer at the end of this chapter whenever you feel stuck in this cycle, or feel free to create your own.

"F" Your Relationships

Relationships are our life's assignments. They provide all the education one could possibly need in a lifetime. This could not be truer in my life. Whether it's romantic, close friends, acquaintances, strangers, or family—your relationships become your classroom every single day. Relationships are our teachers, they are our mirrors, and they are our biggest gifts.

Every teacher has a different style and shows up for us in different ways. Some are here to teach us how to love, to forgive, to have more compassion, to be more loving, to create boundaries, to leave what is not for us any longer, to stick to something even when it's hard, to have more fun, to be more adventurous, to be more attentive or open. The list goes on and on, and so do our interactions and lessons. Since becoming more aware, I feel that every interaction I've had since has taught me something. If we can view every relationship as a teacher and be grateful for the lesson, we will have a much easier and far more enjoyable time in life instead of assuming everyone is supposed to make us feel good or that we're supposed to make them like us. There is very little learning in that, and if that were the case, we'd stop appreciating these people because of the lack of things to contrast and stimulate our minds. Every relationship is an opportunity to come from a loving place and also practice how authenically you can be without judging yourself, them, or the interaction.

It is important, however, to notice when the same type of teacher (that you're not enjoying) keeps showing up for you; for instance, attracting the same type of friend that unloads on you or the boyfriend that puts you on the back burner. Could they be trying to teach you that you need to start speaking up, setting boundaries, and getting clear on what you will and won't accept in your life? Or maybe that no matter how good that guy is, you get jealous and end up sabotaging the relationship? Is this situation a reminder that you need to choose love instead of fear and lack and not feeling enough? How could you use this experience as a mirror reflecting that there may be a need for more self-love, trust, and faith? How could you choose the light and love when it feels so scary, real, and out of control? The courage to choose a different path; to choose love is the miracle and where you gain back your power.

If you continue to attract these teachers, it may be time to start focusing on the lessons you're learning from them and making new choices in order to get a different outcome—or this will be your life on repeat. That could mean you choose to love yourself enough to walk away, or love yourself enough to know your worth and stay.

Grudges, Dislike, Hatred, and Anger

Holding on to anger and grudges is like drinking poison and expecting the other person to die.

—UNKNOWN

When we feel negative feelings toward someone or we're not forgiving someone, we become their slave. We replay the painful event over and over and continue to be abused and victimized by the thought. We start to fantasize about how we would hurt them, get them back, or plead our case. All the while they feel nothing and we're at their mercy. This cycle is the pain and blame prison people sentence themselves to for life and it sucks all the energy out of you.

Even the mildest case of dislike can block us from our joy. We may never feel totally free, but we can get pretty close with a daily forgiveness practice. Sending them love and releasing them to be who they are will free you to do the same. The only way to be free is to release them.

Use one of the prayers at the end of this chapter to help you through challenging moments in your relationships, or create your own.

"F" Your Perfectionist and Procrastinator

Perfectionism is an intellectual's excuse for procrastination.

Don't you love/hate getting called out? For real, perfectionism is stopping so many of us from doing anything. Please hear me when I say if you're waiting for a perfect time, the perfect idea, or for something to be perfected, you will never do anything.

Failure is the successful person's process of elimination. Failing faster is the goal. It doesn't matter how many times you fail, it only matters how fast you come back from the failures.

Perfectionism is paralyzing and perfection doesn't exist. Plus, "perceived perfection" is just so damn boring. Nobody wants to see it anymore. We want to know the entire ugly journey and all the mistakes it took to get there. The only people who are criticizing you and expecting you to be perfect are the perfectionists, and they're not putting their soul's work out to the world out of fear of not being perfect, so their opinions don't matter anyway. Plus they're so damn busy judging their imperfections that they don't even see you. You can put yourself out there and attract your perfect tribe, or you can put who you think you should be out there: "your representative," as Glennon Doyle Melton calls it, and attract a bunch of confused, lost souls, wasting time. Be you and be a magnet for those who are trying to support, connect, and run with you in this lifetime.

> *We are not here to be perfect, we are here to learn.*
> *We are not here to be right, we're here to share an*
> *imperfect human experience.*
> *A lesson learned in public means you're on an*
> *accelerated path—don't be ashamed, be excited*
> *you gained massive growth.*
> *Embrace the perfectly imperfect process.*

"F" the Victims

Before I begin, I want to make sure you know we're talking about different types of victims here. If you have been a victim of brutality or sexual trauma and the wound is still raw, you will require extra self-compassion and time to move through those traumatic feelings. After I was kidnapped and assaulted, I had to feel all of the pain and emotion first in order to be able to come through the other side and understand what I needed to heal and what my process was to release my abuser and free myself of the repeated memory. Please take your time, use the prayers at the end of this chapter, and know that you can be free if you are willing to altar it up, trust, and commit to your peace.

We've all experienced it, whether it's your inner victim or a person in your life who always makes themselves the victim. Playing the role of the victim as a way to justify actions or inactions, not take accountability, or escape from facing fears and problems will keep you stuck. In fact, being a victim or surrounding yourself with them will bury you alive. Bad things happen and they are a part of our story, but letting them define us and form our future becomes self-mutilation.

This is the part where you free yourself . . . If what you're about to read smacks you in the face, feels like I'm slapping you on the wrist, or makes you upset with me, that means you have the biggest opportunity of all to shift into your power. I'm not here for you to like me, I'm here to help you transform. Let me first explain that I am able to understand this lesson so well because I had to forgive my inner victim and release those who are victims around me. I've said it a thousand times, but this is a huge practice for me. The more honest you can get with yourself here, the quicker you can be free.

It's time to "F" your victims if:

> *You think if you're seen as a victim, you don't have to be held accountable for your poor choices or the way you treat people.*
>
> *You can't acknowledge the good or things people do for you (especially on social media) because it would take away from your identity and the attention you get as being the victim of bad luck.*

You believe that if you've been a victim in the past that
you still are.
You feel that somehow a person or event has had the
strength to take your power away.
You practice being the victim daily by either blaming,
complaining, or justifying.

You often say or think the following:

I'm this way because . . .
I can't do that because this horrible thing happened to
me . . .
I can't show up for you because of this . . .
I can't make money because . . .
I can't lose weight because . . .
I'm broken and unworthy because . . .
I'm awful in relationships because . . .
I can't reach my dream because . . .

In order to get your power back, you must forgive and release the person and event you are blaming, and then forgive yourself and bring massive compassion to your inner victim. Remind yourself you don't need this story to get love, attention, or an unfulfilled need met.

The most empowering thing you can do is take a good look at why you are using your "victim story" as a crutch. What fears, discomfort, and pain are you trying to avoid by relying on it? What need are you trying to fill by falling back on this?

You can rest easy knowing there is always a more empowering, compassionate choice that could be made, but we don't choose it out of fear. There is always a way to get a different outcome if you choose to react differently. You must choose to react from ownership and positive action—not from your old victim story. Although this first seems scary, slowly taking steps to overcome your fear and anxiety will actually give you the authentic, loving power and connection you've been yearning for without the victim side effects of pain, isolation, martyrdom, and regression.

Release those who are still playing the victim.

You may have someone in your life that no matter what you do for them they always seem to believe the world is against them and they are always the victim. They are so consumed by this belief that they do everything they can to collect the evidence around that keeps them remaining the victim instead of seeing and focusing on their wins, being grateful for what they do have, and reaching for the thoughts and choices that empower them. They will not unclench the belief that they will just get victimized, taken advantage of, or dealt another shitty hand no matter what they try. "Nothing ever turns out good for me." If you find yourself in any kind of relationship with a victim, odds are you will become their victimizer somehow. They have to stay true to their identity, so they will do everything in their might to make you wrong if you are trying to make their life better.

I've had people in my life that I used to complain about all the time. I would ramble on about how they hurt everyone's feelings and how much of a victim they were no matter what you did for them. It took someone saying "Stop stepping in front of the bus" for me to understand I needed to remove myself from their non-stop poor me, passive-aggressive punishment that had ensued in my life. I realized that you can't fix any person but yourself. All you can do is stop taking the bait and step away.

Release them, send them love, and allow them to show up in a teacher's role for you and decide what boundaries you need to set. These types of people are some of my best teachers of compassion and boundaries.

"F" Your Judgment and Comparison

If you're feeling judged and criticized, it's because you're doing this to yourself, others, or both. How we view others is how we view ourselves. Don't beat yourself up for this. This is completely normal, but it's also the huge reason why we don't go for our dreams and feel so insecure and uncomfortable being ourselves.

The more critical you are of others, the more you think people are criticizing you. The more you judge others, the more evidence you gather that people are judging you. The more you compare yourself, the more you fall short and feel compared.

There is magic to be experienced when you are able to catch this and replace it with appreciation and celebration. When appreciation becomes your practice, you start to see things in yourself for which you feel proud and excited.

When you begin to celebrate the contrast, gifts, and diversity of others—no matter how annoying, weird, or imperfect—you fall in love with the idiosyncrasies of yourself and begin to get excited about the "perfectly imperfect gifts" you have to offer as well.

We are all made of and from the same source energy, so when we separate ourselves from them, cut them down, and judge, we are harming ourselves. This is because we are them, and they exist in us. Their shadow is a part of us that we're not seeing.

When we compare or get jealous, we only feel that because they are reflecting a part of ourselves that we are not allowing ourselves to cultivate and share. When we celebrate them and see that their light is our light, we free ourselves to shine and celebrate our own unique offerings to the world.

My challenge for you is to replace judgment, comparison, or criticism with celebration. State in your mind what's good about them or why being different from you is a great thing.

When you feel hurt, upset, or like you just can't find the strength to forgive, prayer will be your path to freedom.

Next time you are struggling with any of the topics mentioned in this chapter, choose one of these prayers or create your own:

"Creator, I offer this up to You. I'm ready to release this person (or yourself) and be free of this pain. Please give me the strength to see this differently and to choose peace and love."

"Source, give me your holy spirit to help me release this person. I am ready to release them. Please give me the strength to forgive this person. I am willing to see them with love."

A great exercise in forgiveness is to write a letter to yourself or to someone that you have been having trouble forgiving. You won't send the letter; this is just for you. Write down why you felt hurt and how this affected your life. Next, I want you to write from a place of compassion and try to understand why this happened, how this could have come from a place of fear, misunderstanding, lack, etc. on their part. Then tell them what lesson you learned and how this has benefited you. End your letter by telling them you forgive them and wishing them well in the future. Tell them you release them so that you can move forward and stop carrying the pain of this occurrence.

Optional: Do a letter-burning ceremony. Find a safe way to burn the letter that you have written while saying the prayer: "I release you, I am free, you are free. God give me the strength to see you with love."

SOUL ASSIGNMENT:

What is calling for forgiveness in your life right now so you can be free?

What form will this forgiveness take?

How will you practice forgiveness every time this comes up?

TRIBE DISCUSSION:

Start out each discussion by sharing what you're grateful for, excited about, and your answers for the questions above. Then, complete the statement below. Remember to respect time and adhere to tribe agreements.

Something else that came up for me was . . .

REMINDER:

Don't forget to set the appointment for your next tribe meeting and choose what chapter or chapters you will discuss next. (Suggestion: Continue on to read the introduction to section 3 and also chapter 14 on your own and complete the Soul Assignment, but wait to do the Tribe Work together during your next meeting.)

section three

THE NEW WAY OF BELONGING (TO YOURSELF)

Welcome to the New Way of Belonging. This section is dedicated to your own individual self-work within the tribe. You will be discovering exactly who you are and how to change your stories and beliefs around yourself and what you think is possible. It's important now to focus solely on you within the refuge of the tribe because if you can't love and accept yourself, you'll never be able to sop up the decadent blessings relationships bring. The power of working on yourself within a tribe is that it allows you to open up and explore even deeper than you may have alone, knowing when you're in uncharted water and your anchor hits rock bottom—it's attached to a ship and crew who can help pull you back up when you're ready to set sail again.

When I say "belonging" in the book it does not mean trying to fit in. It does not mean changing who you are. It means becoming more of who you are and having the willingness to show the world the real you. Belonging takes forgiveness, bravery, vulnerability, acceptance of our past, uncovering and taking complete ownership of our own magic. Belonging means sharing your light, understanding how to tap into your own inner wisdom and connect to that loving, nurturing, accepting part of yourself. In this section you'll read lessons and do exercises with your tribe to gain tools to uncover and reclaim yourself and your belonging. When you are clear on who you are and have the tools to connect to yourself, you don't worry about belonging because you will know that you do. You won't try to fit in or make people like you because you will carry the energy of certainty, which turns you into a magnet. You will no longer use your relationships and tribes for validation, which will allow you to finally connect in a way that incites lasting relationships based on love and support instead of need, lack, or fear of not being enough. This new way of belonging allows those who were not loving you in an authentic way to remove themselves from your life as well.

In this section you will be using the book the same way as the previous section: reading the chapter, doing the Soul Assignments on your own, and waiting to do the Tribe Work during your scheduled meeting time.

fourteen

WHO ARE YOU?

He walks up slowly, staring into my eyes. It's the kind of stare that only someone who has nothing to lose could give to a TOTAL stranger. "I'm a stand-up comedian . . ." he begins, and pauses while getting more intense with his gaze. He's completely stone-faced, but there is a part of me that senses he is harmless. He's getting closer and now I'm getting a bit uncomfortable. He finishes his joke. "Because I'm standing up." I crack a smile. He has no shoes on and his feet are soiled and black. I observe he's wearing an old, oversized suit coat, dress pants that are about three sizes too big, and a ball cap. Despite the stains and personal invasion of space he's oddly charming and I can't help but be curious about his story, and how he ended up homeless.

"Who are you?" he asks . . . "C'mon, who are you? Who do you think you are?" He just keeps asking me this . . . I am completely blank. *Who am I right now that actually matters to him or that I care to even share?* Nothing is coming up except all I can think to myself is *In this moment I am just love.* He begins saying some judgmental, rude things and I know nothing

I could say would get through to him besides being loving. "Do you know who I am? Who do you think I am?" he asks. At this point I'm getting annoyed and I say, "Right now you are someone I get to flex my love muscle on." Weird answer, I know, but it just came out of my mouth. "Perfect, let me know when we can flex our love muscles together," he says. I bust out laughing because, well, THAT. He laughs and says, "Thank you . . ." My soul interprets his thank-you as me actually seeing him for who he is—a slightly pervy yet funny man with a true desire to make people laugh. My husband comes out in that moment with both of us laughing. We all smile and part ways as he says, "Thanks for keeping me company." "Likewise," I say as I'm still pondering our interaction and his persistent prodding question.

"Who am I?"

When's the last time you were asked that (if ever)? If you know what makes you tick, what makes you happy, fulfilled, sad, mad, etc., you also understand what you need, desire, and enjoy. You can't answer this onion of a question without peeling back layers, wanting to look away, close your eyes, and possibly shed some tears trying to figure it out.

WHAT'S YOUR TITLE

I find myself sitting in a sea of people all gathered together inside the LA Convention Center in hopes to take our lives and business to new levels. I love learning and am an eternal student of life, so I eat this stuff up. The facilitator is tall, good-looking, captivating, and ever-so-slightly intimidating, so we are all listening intently. We're talking about why we have the desire for certain things and titles and why we have the motivations we have and he asks the question "Whose love did you crave the most growing up?" I sit there thinking for a minute . . . Well, I think I craved my mom's love the most, for some reason. Then he asks, "Who do you think you needed to be in order to get that love that you craved?" This is where it got interesting. My brain answers quickly—"I needed to be perfect."

I sat there with my jaw open having this realization that I had spent the beginning part of my life trying to be the impossible and feeling like a failure. What did "perfect" even mean to me? A list ran through my head—quiet, agreeable, pure, Godly, helpful, good, clean, never rock the boat, don't draw attention and keep opinions to yourself, don't swear, drink, smoke, and for the love of all that is holy, don't even think about sex until marriage. Yes, *that* was what I thought her idea of perfect meant.

Even though my mother never said all of these things, I am one of those people (empaths) that feels all the feelings of others around me. I made up this title of "perfect" as who I needed to be in order to help her, not add to her stress and be accepted by her. I remember always wanting to do anything I could to take away her anxiety and pain, but no matter how perfect I was, I could never make it better.

Perfect = Love. Love = Happiness.

I realized later that this story with my mother was just a small piece compared to the impossible standard of perfection I felt was expected of me in my religion, and this hidden imperfect life was eating me alive. I moved out when I was eighteen, not because I didn't love my mother or family—I loved them dearly—

but because I couldn't fathom them finding out who I was and I couldn't lie anymore. I needed to see if I could find myself, find peace, and figure out who I was under all this fear, anxiety, shame, and guilt.

Having moved to a college town, where education, careers, and titles were the Alpha and the Omega of conversation and student life, I began to observe that titles seemed to be able to acquire attention and importance. I felt so uneducated and forgettable, and I knew I would need a title in order to get the attention and love I was craving in this new flashy adult world I was in. I would gain acceptance into this new tribe through titles, one way or another.

I became a title hunter. My external title, *waitress*, and internal title, *not smart enough*, had me feeling embarrassed and insecure. I wanted people to look at me, see me, need me, crave me. I was starved for attention and fulfillment. I was convinced a title would finally make me feel whole. I spent the next decade trying to define who I was with a title.

Fast-forward thirteen years and a whole lot of self-work, life experience, and rock bottoms later, and I really felt I had figured "it" out. I felt detached from my old beliefs that our titles brought us the love and attention and was living my purpose. I loved helping people. I gave advice, and I helped them fix their problems whenever, however I could. A few years in, I felt completely drained, disconnected, and like I needed a new business plan, so I hired a coach by the name of Gabrielle Bernstein. It took one call to realize my burnout was coming from my need to fulfill the identity of a new title I had created in order to feel like I belong, like I was worthy, and like I was loved.

"What's been coming up for you?" Gabby asks. Just when I'm so ready to jot down some epic biz strategies, my insides come gushing out as my vocal cords take over, releasing some personal fear that has *nothing to do with my business*. I could feel what felt like an emotional back-up coming out. I hadn't felt safe enough to share that in so long for fear of being a burden and not adding value that I began to uncontrollably spew out how lonely and drained I was feeling, despite the fact that I was doing exactly what I loved. I had been volunteering, speaking, starting new projects, and running successful programs. But I was physically, mentally, and spiritually tapped out. I was heading toward a rock bottom.

"Why do you think you feel lonely and drained?" Gabby asked. "Good question," I said. Though I remember thinking, *If I knew the answer, I would tell you!* I could feel myself finding ways to deflect—I could ask her questions about herself, or maybe I could ask how she is, except this was *my* coaching call and she was not willing to talk about her. *Crap.* In silence, my mind began racing.

Oh my gosh, I have nowhere to go. I have nothing to fix. What do I do? I can't cry. This is weird. I hate this! Why do I have a coach, again? I'm just fine! How can I deflect this and ask about her? I feel so self-centered talking about my problems. Why can't we just skip this and talk business? This is so dumb. Oh my gosh, I'm totally going to cry, and she's going to think I'm a weak, needy, whiny bitch! But I'm all good, right?! What is happening? I can't escape! Help me!

"Tears are clarifying," she eventually said. The floodgates opened. I started choking out words while wiping tears and snot from my face. I began telling her about how I am "a fixer," and I had no idea that I had all of this emotion around it. "It's who I am. I think I just need to find more ways to get in front of more people to fix more problems. If I could do that, I'd stop feeling tired and lonely." At this point, I was crying harder because I was so embarrassed about the sharing and the crying. She then pointed out that I was relying on my clients and audience to make me feel recharged, loved, and connected. I was pouring everything I had into them, but never giving myself a space to ask for help, share my needs, recharge, connect, fill up, or get vulnerable. "How's that working?" she asked.

It wasn't. All of a sudden it was like a light went on. On that call, I realized that I avoid people I can't help because I don't feel valuable or needed unless I can fix something for them. If I can't help someone, they don't need me and I have no value. Therefore, I am only drawn to people I feel I can help, and if these are the only people I am spending time with, then I am only giving and never receiving, recharging, or connecting. Unbeknownst to me I was always a "fixer."

My title of the "fixer" can be traced all the way back to my childhood. As a little girl, I watched my parents stress over finances, over family, and over my older sister's teenage debacles. The less stress I created, the more lovable I was, and if I could help, clean, or fix something, the more valuable I became to those around me. It was then that I decided to rock the boat as little as possible—or at least if I had a problem, I'd stuff it down deep and keep it hidden from them. I grew into a woman who made sure people knew they could count on me for anything, and I decided that I would figure out all my problems on my own. I hadn't been letting anyone in on what wasn't working in my life—not even myself. I wasn't asking for help or even a listening ear. Instead, I was self-sustaining under a title that was creating waves of inner turmoil. I was lonely. I was tired. I was not connecting to anyone as a result of my inability to go to that scary place of vulnerability where I'd have to share myself (and possibly cry) with other people and allow them to help me. Moving forward, I would have to ask myself if people would still love me if I rocked the boat and asked for what I needed, because I was not okay and now I had a choice to stop pretending that I was.

So let me ask, what title have you given yourself? Go ahead and list a few of your own.

Need a kick-start? Do any of these sound like they might fit?

Caretaker
Reliable One
Drama Queen
Hot Head
Boss
Shy
Anxious
Class Clown
Intellectual
Perfectionist
Peacemaker

Breadwinner
Screwup
Responsible One
Mother
Wife
Sister

Whatever title or identity you have knowingly (or unknowingly) anointed yourself with, with a little work and the right tribe, and the right questions, you will be free of it. So it's time to do some checking in by asking the right questions and taking the right actions that will free us and move us toward our truth and away from our fear. It's time to discover you.

SOUL ASSIGNMENT:

Who did you believe you needed to be growing up in order to be accepted and loved?
Who do you believe you need to be now in order to feel happy and accepted?
What does having your identity attached to this title make you do that is no longer working for you?

TRIBE DISCUSSION:

Start out each discussion by sharing what you're grateful for, excited about, and your answers for the questions above. Then, complete the statement that follows. Remember to respect time and adhere to tribe agreements.

Something else that came up for me was . . .

REMINDER:

Don't forget to set the appointment for your next tribe meeting and choose what chapter or chapters you will discuss next. (Suggestion: Continue on to read chapter 15 on your own and complete the Soul Assignment, but wait to do the Tribe Work together during your next meeting.)

fifteen

RECLAIMING *HER*

And the day came when the risk to remain tight in the bud was more painful than the risk it took to blossom.

—ANAÏS NIN

When I was little, I remember being a beam of rainbow-y sunshine. I had big eyes that looked at everything with possibility, and a contagious laugh that often ended on a snort, which made me laugh even harder at my own jokes. Even at a young age I remember feeling a fierceness, a knowing, a certainty of who I was and that I was here to do big things. I waved my weirdo flag high for all to see. I didn't care where I was or what was going on, because I would turn every situation into a good time because I knew I was the good time. "Playing" was my M.O. Years passed and I hid this version of me away, but deep down I felt like she was still in there.

As I reached my late twenties and started really putting

myself out in the public eye and striving for my goal of having a career in the health and mindset space, I knew challenges and criticism lay ahead on this unfamiliar road. I was convinced I had to become serious to be taken seriously. This form of self-preservation led me to hold back in a variety of ways when presented with an opportunity to connect with people—from my humor to how I dressed, I was buttoned-up in every aspect. I wasn't having any fun, I was having trouble trusting myself and others. I honestly wasn't really sure who I was anymore.

Fast-forward to 2014 and I'm sitting at dinner after finishing up one of the biggest milestones of my life. I faced my biggest fears in order to put on my first three-hundred-person event (The Bliss Project), and all of a sudden I get a surprise right hook, "You spend so much time telling other people to follow their soul, but you don't do it yourself. When is the last time you've done something fun or just for you?" she said to me. *She* being a friend of mine named Jackie, whom I've known for quite a while. Jackie's notoriously honest, or in other words, blunt. Normally I love this about her, but on this day, I was just pissed.

I sat there thinking, *I'm sorry, did I ask you for this feedback?* I was expecting more like "Congratulations on achieving everything you ever wanted!" I mean, I was actually achieving my goals, which felt good and was more than I can say for a lot of people, so where does she even get off saying something like that?! Now, because I've had time to digest this, let me just sandwich this between two slices of whole grain truth—on the one slice, she would not have asked this question if I had not been complaining about how tired and drained I was from working nonstop; and on the second, I had shared with her that I felt so off, lonely, and unfulfilled after this event and couldn't figure out why.

As much as I wanted to deem Jackie a completely ignorant boob in that moment, her words pierced straight to my soul. After all, Jackie and I first connected over lusty dreams of surf adventures and all things soul-drenched and nonsensical. I couldn't stop thinking about what she said and noticing how over the last few years I had stopped doing certain things that made me really happy. I had totally rejected ginormous parts of myself while on this path to success.

My life consisted only of working, meditating, self-development programs, books, events, podcasts, etc. . . . I had to constantly be learning and getting better to become the successful woman I wanted to be, right? I had to grind and hustle to be that empowered "Girl Boss"! I had to know it all, work harder, and become some sort of guru to be taken seriously. I had no time to play! Isn't this what everyone else was doing? Shouldn't I feel happy if I'm reaching my goals? Shouldn't I feel alive and fulfilled now that I'm doing what I dreamed of?

Looking back, I didn't lose touch with that awesome little girl; I pushed her down. I covered up her mouth. I told her people would make fun of her and think she was stupid, weird, awkward, or attention hungry. I loved her too much to let people make fun of her, so she had to go. I had no choice but to put her in shackles and smother her light to keep her hidden safely, where no one could see her. I had completely forgotten how to be the real me.

GATO ENOJADO

The thing about your soul is that no matter how much you try to deny it or put it under a basket, it becomes like a *Gato Enojado*, otherwise known as an *Angry Cat*. You could pile all your belongings on top of that basket, but she's just going to claw, screech, and scratch every square inch of that thing looking for a way out. There is no quitting, only total destruction or freedom. Your choice, free the *gato* or be forever *enojado* . . .

When you can no longer carry the pain and deal with the damage that betraying yourself causes, you'll make the choice to choose you.

> *If you bring forth what is within you, what you bring forth will save you. If you do not bring forth what is within you, what you do not bring forth will destroy you.*
> —GOSPEL ACCORDING TO THOMAS

Okay, Braveheart, put on your best kilt, because today is the day we reclaim *HER*.

For me, reclaiming my little, hilarious, brilliant, wild weirdo, aka my soul, meant that I had to sit down and get to know her all over again. It had been a while and I wasn't even sure what made her feel alive or motivated her. My job was to be inquisitive about anything that lit her up . . . If I could start figuring out the things, places, and people she loves, then there was no way our paths would not cross frequently if I went to those places, did those things, and surrounded myself with those people, right?

This was my focus: Find and stay close to the things that make me feel alive. Alive, to me, meant anything other than tired and depressed. Your soul doesn't care if you're comfortable. She cares if you're on your path to becoming fully you. BTW— becoming fully you is the ultimate bliss, so don't go wigging on me over some discomfort and unfamiliarity. It's no worse than what you're already feeling denying your soul. The difference is, the discomfort you experience from following your soul has a reward on the other side, and the discomfort you get from remaining the same earns you a membership to the monthly "Whine and (kick to the) Nuts Club." You can't escape pain, so choose the pain that has a reward attached to it. Listen, I promise YOU that you're more than ready for this. Hand on heart . . . Now say it with me, "I'm ready to be free."

The more you tune in, the more she speaks. Sometimes she's clear, sometimes it seems she is speaking in tongues. A good rule of thumb is if you feel any of the following, you are definitely going to explore it and ask deeper questions. Here's how I translate her voice when she speaks to me:

> *Curiosity: She's nudging to explore it deeper.*
> *Quickened breath: She's whispering, this will be good.*
> *Goose bumps: She's telling me this feels like truth.*
> *Heart explosions: She's letting me know it's going to be fun.*
> *Anxious butterflies: We chest bump and high-five. This means she is excited for her next debut and there is something awesome on the other side.*

When you are doing what you love, when you lose track of space and time, when you feel connected, when who you are being is aligned with who you feel you are intrinsically, when you're following your nudges, investigating your curiosities, when you feel pulled rather than pushing yourself, this is when you're in "flow" as they say and she's got the wheel. This is where you get to loosen that kung-fu grip and trust you're in good hands. But I'm telling you she takes a totally different direction than you ever think she's going to. She's obsessed with old pot-holed roads, narrow lanes, winding mountain trails, and taking the long scenic route. But once in a while she'll surprise you and put you on a rocket ship going full throttle—if this happens you count your blessings and grab a Dramamine, cuz you're on the fast track.

Don't get it twisted. Your soul is not just a "Yes (wo)man." She is a fierce CEO and when you put her in charge she can't help but cut through the bullshit quickly to get things done. She sees what is mission critical for the highest good. This is where it gets murky for our minds and this human personality of ours, because the highest good does not always feel, well . . . good. We are souls having a human experience and we are all just doing the very best we can. What is true for you now, may not work going forward. Allowing yourself to follow the ever-evolving truth of your soul to the highest good and bring it forth is the path to freedom. That's what you're about to learn to do.

If you've been walking around your whole life with your soul in a dark corner or stuffed into a girdle this may feel a little too loosey goosey and exposed for you, but in time you'll feel so comfortable with your soul that you will trust it to make all the decisions for you.

Later I'm going to share some amazing tools to tap into this soul/higher power connection even more, but first we need a foundation. Let's start with some questions, and remember re-uniting can feel like a first date, so she's probably not gonna give it all up right away. You have to get to know her all over again, take interest, treat her right, see what excites her, and then . . . Well, let's just say it is a million times better than fireworks. So let's ease into it, shall we? Just drinks?

SOUL ASSIGNMENT:

What lights her up?
What is something she wants to stop doing?
Where does she like to hang out?
What kinds of people does she come out around the most?
When does she feel most free?

TRIBE DISCUSSION:

Start out each discussion by sharing what you're grateful for, excited about, and your answers for the questions above. Then, complete the statement below. Remember to respect time and adhere to tribe agreements.

Something else that came up for me was . . .

REMINDER:

Don't forget to set the appointment for your next tribe meeting and choose what chapter or chapters you will discuss next.
(Suggestion: Continue on to read chapter 16 on your own and
complete the Soul Assignment, but wait to do the Tribe Work
together during your next meeting.)

sixteen

MEET YOUR SOUL

You don't have a soul. You are a soul. You have a body.

—C. S. LEWIS

I'm a little woo-woo. Let's just get that out there. Woo-woo meaning that I'm one of those people who doesn't believe the propaganda that we've been told about being stuck in our less-than-desirable circumstances. I think differently, speak differently, and live life differently than most and I don't believe it's normal to be unhappy and struggle. Was I always this way? Heck no! My old self is still over here like, "I can't believe this shit really works!" Don't get me wrong, I still feel pain, have suck-ass days, feel scared, anxious, and get pissed, but the amount of time I spend in these states has become pretty damn small. I believe in trying unconventional things that some may think to be weird, too hard, too easy, or too stupid in order to get unconventional results.

If you've gotten this far in this book, you are receiving a blaring, life-shifting memo from your soul. She's ready to connect you to something BIG, so it doesn't matter if you feel like you are ready or not. She's already proven she will guide you to what you need, and now it's time to trust her. I'm just here to teach you how to be able to hear and understand her better.

Here's the deal, this whole figuring out who your tribe is, who you are, and what will lead you to your bliss THING, is going to be a whole lot easier if we can ever so slightly lean into, or if you want to fast track this puppy—GO ALL IN on believing you are connected to something far bigger than you. Because there is no way I could have success or fulfillment if I did not believe and have faith I am supported by this greater connection.

It doesn't matter what you call *it*—God, Universe, Spirit, Source, Divine, Buddha, The Great Unicorn-Kitty in the Sky . . . You automatically get plugged in the second you are willing to believe in *it*. Now, just so I don't lose you to semantics, I want you to know that I will be (and have been) interchanging the above names and you fill in whatever you need in order to get the message throughout these pages. Don't miss the message because it's in a different language. It doesn't matter what language you speak, you will feel the intention behind the words. Remember, "Eat the Fruit and Spit Out the Seeds."

So let me ask you . . . Are you willing to challenge your beliefs (or maybe non-beliefs)? Whose advice have you been taking? Would you take financial advice from a broke financial advisor? No? So why then would you take life advice from someone who isn't thriving, happy, or doesn't do what you hope to do? Just sayin'. Only listen to 'em if you want their results. So here I am, slammin' this blissed-out Kool-Aid, and I'm laughing, creating, loving, expressing, and experiencing a life I never could have dreamed of unless I was open. The question isn't if you're meant for an epic life, it's when will you accept that you are? You *are* meant to experience miracles daily. The only variable is you. Once you step out of that suffocating fear closet, then oh baby, I've got what you need and so does your tribe. When you commit to love, your blessings and earth angels show up in droves—get ready.

Let's work on unfucking your journey and clearing any misery torpedoes that may be pelting you right now. Do I have your attention yet? It all comes down to choosing love. In any given moment we can choose love or we can choose fear. However, Source does not speak in anything but love, so we must learn how to choose love over fear. Choosing love is what allows us to stay on the path that guides us to what is best for us individually.

When we choose love, we feel good, happy, aligned. When we choose fear, we feel anxious, scared, alone. So it should be pretty easy to choose love at all times, right? I mean who would actually choose to feel bad? The answer? We all do. We get so used to choosing what we see others choosing and believing what the majority believe that fear can become our default setting until we reprogram to a different one. It is so important that we learn how to translate what is real (love) for you, because much of the world operates on fear. When we can start to choose love instead of the old patterns we have been choosing, we are gonna shift, baby, shift! With your willingness to work on choosing love and building your tribe, you just became a part of the answer. It's time to elevate.

YOUR SOUL'S CONNECTION

The soul has been described in many ways that all boil down to the "I" or personality that inhabits the physical body, the voice of deep inner knowing that is your direct connection to your higher power/source.

The book *Conversations with God* by Neale Donald Walsch explains that our soul already knows who it is.

"Your soul knows all there is to know all the time. There is nothing hidden to it. Yet knowing is not enough. The soul seeks to experience itself."

The book goes on to share that the soul's job is to help guide you (the personality) to the experiences that it needs in order to become what it knows it is in the physical realm. Its job is not to guide you only to happy and joyful experiences. Its job is to guide you to the experiences it NEEDS. The soul only knows how to evolve and grow because that is its job.

Because your soul is unlike anyone else's, we cannot look to others to understand how we personally experience our connection, and this is what we are going to start exploring together so you can define yours. Each of our souls is as individual as snowflakes and has a unique spiritual connection to your higher power.

It's the desire to stay comfortable that stops us from growing into why our soul is here. We often spend our days feeling totally conflicted, wondering if we are making the right decisions in our life. The reason for that is our soul guides us to what we need, which is most often what is not familiar and outside of our current skill set. These things translate into uncertainty and discomfort. We have spent our entire lives learning how to avoid pain, so when it becomes necessary to grow, this is when our ability to translate our soul's language is super helpful in knowing what pain or experience is necessary for our growth and what is not.

Decoding the Language of Your Soul

Something really rad happens when we learn to understand our soul's language. We become our own best guru and teacher because our soul lets us know where Source is directing us.

Remember the movie *A Christmas Story*, when the main character, Ralphie, drinks gallons of Ovaltine so he can get an Orphan Annie Secret Society decoder pin only to find the simple message . . . "Be Sure to Drink Your Ovaltine"? When you start understanding how to decode your soul, you watch how the pieces fall together even when things fall apart, and like Ralphie's decoder, our soul is always trying to give us clues on some pretty common-sense things that would bring us bliss. But since common sense is NOT always common practice, it's time to "Ralphie" the shit out of your soul, aka decode that mother.

Our soul uses a few different modalities to speak. No way is better or more special than another. However you "hear" your soul is how your personality will best understand it. Your soul speaks the loudest and speaks first. It's usually quick in its delivery and means of showing up. This method in which your soul speaks to you needs to be understood and paid attention to because your practical mind is loud and takes over immediately after the initial answer or feeling and we often confuse the two if we are not fine-tuning this skill. Your soul likely speaks to you through one or more of the following ways:

Feelings

Thoughts

Audible Voices

Visions

People

Signs

SOUL TALK

Our soul, like our higher power, has so many different names—intuition, inner guide, GPS, etc.—many of which I interchange throughout this book. But know that whatever you call your soul, it can either be the greatest source of pain and suffering or your path to bliss, all depending on if you listen to it or not. In fact, chances are if you've been ignoring your soul it's led you through some sketchy neighborhoods, where you broke down and had to walk your ass ten miles back to town, in the winter, in the dark, with no jacket, hangry as hell. *But why?* Because it will keep doing whatever it needs to do in order to cause you enough pain to finally get your attention! Your soul doesn't care if you are surrounded by pretty pink clouds and Care Bears on your journey, it cares about the outcome of your life, the richness of your experiences, your truth, your wisdom, and the evolution of you. I want to clarify right now that even when you are listening to your soul it won't always feel good at first. The difference is, when it's a soul-guided decision, it will feel like freedom, clarity, and truth on the other side.

The only certain thing you can count on is that your soul is going to speak to you until you listen. Its job is to give you whatever feelings and experiences you need in order to get aligned with your higher purpose. Just like the old saying goes, "What you resist, persists." If you choose to keep ignoring it, or numbing it out, it is going to keep delivering that same nasty-feeling message, cycle, or pattern until you wake the fuck up and figure out what message it's trying to deliver to you.

Let's all acknowledge our soul and that it has been speaking to us since the beginning. Can you think back to a time when you said any of these things?

> *"I knew this was going to happen."*
> *"I knew I shouldn't have done that!"*
> *"This just feels right to me."*
> *"Something just doesn't feel right."*
> *"I am so drained around that person."*
> *"I find my answers when I'm in silence or walking in
>   nature."*
> *"When I'm doing what I love, it's like life just flows."*

So now you know you've never been alone and since you're now aware and awake to your inner guide let's learn to listen in for your bigger purpose. Unfortunately many people will continue to sleepwalk, and their soul will just deliver jab after jab, until the end of their lives and they lay bruised, and heavy with regret.

Now it's time to start choosing alignment. You are going to learn to observe how the voice of your soul is trying to communicate with you and what it feels like when it does. To sharpen this skill, try to sit quietly for a few minutes daily. Ask questions about anything you need guidance on in your life and then be patient and listen.

SOUL ASSIGNMENT:

Recall a time when you felt guided by an internal voice or a time when you had a gut feeling trying to tell you something. Explain the experience.

> *How did your soul's communication show up? Feelings, voices in your mind, thoughts, signs, etc.*
> *Where in your body did this feeling show up?*
> *What does it feel like when you are in alignment with your soul?*
> *What does it feel like when you are out of alignment with your soul?*

Close your eyes, put your hand on your heart, and ask your soul to have you feel what YES feels like. Now, ask your soul what NO feels like.

Try asking your soul a question that you are unsure of using these skills and observe and see if you can understand what your feelings are trying to offer you.

TRIBE DISCUSSION:

Start out each discussion by sharing what you're grateful for, excited about, and your answers for the questions above. Then, complete the statement below. Remember to respect time and adhere to tribe agreements.

Something else that came up for me was . . .

REMINDER:

Don't forget to set the appointment for your next tribe meeting and choose what chapter or chapters you will discuss next. (Suggestion: Continue on to read chapter 17 on your own and complete the Soul Assignment, but wait to do the Tribe Work together during your next meeting.)

seventeen

WHAT'S YOUR STORY?

Owning your story is the bravest thing you will ever do.
—BRENÉ BROWN

So, what's your story? Add "doll face" to the end of that sentence and it sounds like a 1940s pickup line that would be answered in a smoky bar over some extra-extra-dirty martinis. Depending on your perspective of your life, your story could be told in an infinite number of ways. There is the story you tell about your life to someone you're trying to "pitch" for an opportunity or a new job. There is the story you tell when you are connecting on a deep soul level to another human being. There is the story you share while you're sitting in your therapist's office. Everyone: the hairstylist, your bestie, your parents—even your coffee barista—is going to get a different story from you, and it all depends upon how you feel, your outlook, or your end goal. The same thing happens when you're "pitching" or selling something to yourself in your mind. What I'm saying is that you are always choosing the angle to make your story fit your desired outcome. We do this every day from the second we wake up. We view ourselves, our day, and our tasks through the lenses that we decide to put on that morning, so it's important you understand how to see and complete each story in a way that is beneficial to your desired outcome of your life.

If I'm telling my story, and I focus on the good in my life, I will tell you about a girl who loved to laugh, play, experience life, had a few struggles and hardships that she later chose to turn into her strengths. This version makes me feel pretty great about my life—even the difficult times. If I'm feeling bad or maybe caught in comparison and I focus on the sad parts of my life, I will tell you a sob story about growing up with few friends, teasing, and intense loneliness. This is the version that makes me feel like I missed out on my childhood and my life has been stacked against me. If I focus on the not so pleasant moments, I'll tell you about trauma, depression, loss, drama, the debilitating anxiety, and the fears that came from it all. This version makes me feel helpless, hopeless, and paralyzed by an uncertain, scary world. So if all of these are my "stories," what's the *real* story?

Trick question—it's all made up! Yes, all of it. "Lori, what the F do you mean? I've been through some very real things and I kinda think you're a D-bag for even saying that." If it's all made up, what's it all for? Herein lies the bazillion-dollar question. What is it all for? Why did I have to go through that? What is the meaning? Why do bad things happen to good people? What do I do with all of this? Why am I here?

Let me answer that waterfall of questions with a few questions of my own. What do you want it all to be for? What do you want it all to mean? How could you create a meaning that is so empowering that it moves you to do and become everything you desire?

In this chapter, we're going to loosen the grip on the story that has been driving your current identity that you believe is YOU. The way you view your entire life is most likely coming from a disempowering event or two that has a death grip on you, and it's causing a slight fog over your whole life. Most likely you may still have people in your life that feed and grow your old story, because it is a part of their story they are death gripping for themselves as well. If you are able to grow past it, that means they would be able to as well and that just isn't in their comfort zone, so . . . we go into fear and survival modes and try to reinforce these beliefs to each other, allowing everyone to stay in the life boat even though land is just a swim away.

WHAT IS A STORY?

First let's take the definition of the word. Story (n.): an account of imaginary or real people and events told for entertainment.

A "story" is also our account of an event that took place, aka a memory file we pull from whenever we go to make a decision. These stories say our past is in control of our present. Many of us can recall bad memories from our past, but instead of seeing these memories as singular occurrences from which we learn, we turn our past circumstances into our present identity. This identity then becomes the story of who we are, and the story becomes a belief. These beliefs then become our identity and our future.

Your own stories—the positive and negative—have become the foundation of your identity. And unfortunately the negative stories are the first to pop up in a new situation that's out of your comfort zone and the voice of stories past sounds like this:

> *Who do you think you are to do that?*
> *Why would you try that?*
> *You're not worthy of love!*
> *You're not smart enough!*
> *What if they find out you don't know all the answers?*
> *You're a fraud!*
> *It has never worked out before and it won't work out*
>   *now!*
> *Don't get your hopes up.*

These are all things you have been told or you have heard. Whatever they are, I'm positive you can find plenty of evidence to support your negative story, but it's now time to stop.

Let's take a walk down memory lane so we can take a peek at what kind of negative stories you were told growing up. Chances are, most of us have learned how to view the world as our parents did, and they did their best with what they learned from their parents and then their parents' parents. We may want to consider that these stories and beliefs are outdated or totally untrue.

Growing up you may have heard "life's a bitch and then you die" from people in your life. If you heard it enough, it becomes as true as "the sky is blue." If "life's a bitch" is a core belief, then how do you think you will view circumstances throughout your life? Will you focus on the things that go right? Or will you focus on how unfair this short life is? As humans, we naturally search for evidence to support our beliefs, and we will always find EXACTLY what we are looking for.

What you are looking for is what you will find.

A couple years back, when I first moved to California, we took a Hollywood, open-air bus tour. Our guide was quite witty. He was an aspiring comedic actor and this was his side job. Bus tours allowed him to practice making people laugh while getting paid to do it. Brilliant, right? He made us play games the whole time as he embellished stories and made cracks at the lavish L.A. lifestyles. "Black Range Rovers are the taxicabs of L.A.," he told us at the beginning of the tour. He challenged each of us to yell, throw our hands up, and make a big deal whenever we spotted one, and had us guess how many black Range Rovers we'd see. Some people guessed as many as in the twenties, which was as high as the guesses got. After many screams of "BLACK RANGE ROVER!" we had counted almost a hundred. What's my point? I don't think I would have even noticed one Range Rover during the bus tour if I hadn't been looking for one. Now, ask me how many silver Toyotas I saw and I would say zero. Silver Toyotas were not the cars I was focusing on, despite silver Toyotas being one of the most popular cars on the road.

× × ×

At my annual event, The Bliss Project, one could argue that the women sitting in the audience going through the exercises and group breakouts would all be having the same experience and would have a similar story to tell about it, correct? That couldn't be further from the truth.

Jennifer's story is that she has incurable social anxiety and she is totally uncomfortable, but was invited by a friend. She doesn't really want to be in the room and has already told her friend that nothing will work and she can't be helped. Jennifer leaves feeling upset and with the story that she was put in an undesirable situation (in her opinion) because her friend should have known her anxiety would flare up in a setting like this.

Amy is also uncomfortable, fearful, and feels awkward. She feels the same debilitating social anxiety described by the other woman, but the difference is that she has chosen to not let it stop her from doing the things she wants and chooses to believe she can help it with perspective and practice. Although she is in terrible discomfort, she is able to see it as the exact experience she needs to get more used to being in social situations and uses it to break through. Afterward, she is so proud of herself for sticking to it, and feels a deep sense of accomplishment, reward, and connection to the other women, all because of her perspective and choice to use it to grow. She may not be free yet, but she now knows it can slowly get better with exposure and practice.

Jennifer's story is that she still can't connect or break through due to this anxiety. She believes to her core that it holds her back from all of her goals in life and allows it to stop her before she even begins. The story she plays in her head is "I can't accomplish my goals because of my anxiety." Amy has the same anxiety but believes that it can be a tool to connect to other women feeling the same way and uses her experience to share how you can still accomplish your goals if you are willing to sit in the discomfort and view it as the experience you need to get better. The story playing in Amy's head is "I will accomplish my goals and use my anxiety to help me connect and grow. I will view it as my message to the world that you can thrive with it."

Let's explore the flip side of this. Take for example someone who was raised to always look on the bright side and to be grateful for all the things in their life, no matter what happens. We meet these people all the time. Things always seem to go right for them, and they never have a complaint or worry. They get categorized as people with "charmed lives" or accused of always being "too positive." But when you look closer, you will start to see that it's all about where they put their focus—or don't put their focus.

Few of those with "charmed lives" are unscathed. In fact, you'd be shocked by the unfortunate circumstances these people have experienced. The difference is that they focus so much on the positive elements of their life that they are not defined by the negative elements. They refuse to take on the identity of a victim and in place of that choose to seek greatness and become the hero of their own lives. These people find as much evidence of love and goodness around them as those who are playing the "bad, hard, and unfair card" are finding roadblocks and failures around them. The big lesson we can learn from these people with "charmed lives," these seekers of greatness: We are not what has happened to us, but instead we are what we focus on, what we think of, what we speak of—and what we seek.

Unfortunately, it's not as easy as it seems to throw out our old stories and replace them with new. Each story comes with a personal meaning that we've applied to it, a meaning that we still cling to. It's human nature to be a meaning-seeking machine. Things must have a reason or purpose, so we add *meaning* to things that have happened. What would our lives be without meaning, right? Why would a relationship, a marriage, the love of a child, spiritual beliefs, and morals matter if they held no meaning?

The trouble we can run into as meaning-seeking machines is that we have our "seek mode" on a setting that may not be to our benefit. We interpret meaning in our own way and it is typically very one-sided. We miss giant pieces of the puzzle and because we may never get them from other people, we must learn how to fill in these pieces for ourselves so we can feel complete. The only part of the story that matters is the meaning we choose to apply to it after the occurrence has happened. There will always be events in our lives that are painful, unpleasant, and tragic. The only way to move forward and find peace is to rewrite the story and complete the incompletes of the story in a way that works for you, "truth" or not. Remember, truth is made up. It's what you choose it to mean. Choose a truth that empowers you, inspires you, and gives your life meaning.

FIND THE VALUE IN YOUR STORIES

So what now? "You summon all the courage you require" (Alexander Hamilton), and change the direction of your life by changing the perception of our stories. True, bad things do happen, but now (as we learn to apply our own meaning), we have a choice. Choose to see bad things as bad things or choose to see bad things as opportunities to learn and grow. I even hate saying "bad things" because those become some of the best things at times. Don't get me wrong, some of these bad things are far more painful than others, but each one can be seen as growth, and when we share our painful moments with others, we can help them move past their bad memory files and the stories that have them stuck. Our stories no longer have the power over us when we can appreciate the value, perspective, compassion, and strength they have added to our lives.

Even in the darkest, saddest story, you will find that there is something that can help save someone else. Somewhere, there is a child or adult who is waiting to hear your story so that they can be inspired to be the hero of their own lives and in the lives of others. If you are brave enough to share your story, such an act of greatness can help save the life and dreams of someone else. When *you* overcome the odds, you create hope and your story creates a ripple effect.

Let me explain how the brain works. We think up to seventy thousand thoughts per day, and 70–80 percent of them are negative. I want you to start seeing your brain for what it really is—a command center for your body and your life. It tells you how to act, how to react, and what to attract. Therefore, what you think *is* your reality. Has this sunk in yet? Take a minute to ponder what I'm saying. *Your* thoughts are commanding your life. Your life is exactly as you have created in your mind. It can't get better until you believe it will. Don't get mad at your brain or how beautifully you are made, after all it's just trying to pull from your experiences in your environment to help you. Except one experience is NOT enough data to build a set of beliefs that will work in a giant world full of people with completely different experiences. I'm about to teach you in the next chapter exactly how to rewrite your stories so they work for you, and in order to do that we first have to call out the "fiction" we've been choosing.

Let me share how to start winning this war in your brain. We can't create a new life without thinking we are just as blessed, lucky, worthy, and capable as the next gal. Yes, I said lucky. Even my most embarrassing, "I would die if someone found out" moments have given me some kind of gift of perspective, relatability factor, or just some insane motivation on what I will never, ever choose again—especially later on the journey when there is more on the line.

What stories have created your life? What stories are destroying your life? What are the stories robbing you of your future or that are pulling you back into the past? This is going to help you unlock any last shackles from your old stories. In order to completely free yourself, you must take ownership of the fact that your story is also serving you . . . I know that seems crazy, but this is the secret sauce to being able to rewrite a legendary story. Holding on to our stories allows us to stay in our comfort zone because we believe that we "can't," which means we don't have to do that thing that could get us rejected, publicly humiliated, or that we may have to do some really tough stuff like leave relationships or "hurt" someone's feelings.

SOUL ASSIGNMENT:

In order to figure out the most pressing story to begin with, you must determine the one story that stops you from taking that first step toward feeling better or that first step toward your goal. What is the story on repeat that keeps you from a life you love?

Example: My story that was on repeat was "I'm not smart and I have anxiety. These things keep me from doing anything I desire. I will have a panic attack and people will think I'm a fraud. They will find out that I am a failure." This was the story that kept me from getting any job I wanted, it kept me from taking action on my dreams, and the hardest truth of all . . . it kept me from having to get uncomfortable and doing the work it took to be free.

Now write down your story.

Who would you be without this story?

TRIBE DISCUSSION:

Start out each discussion by sharing what you're grateful for, excited about, and your answer for the question above. Then, complete the statement below. Remember to respect time and adhere to tribe agreements.

Something else that came up for me was . . .

REMINDER:

Don't forget to set the appointment for your next tribe meeting and choose what chapter or chapters you will discuss next.
(Suggestion: Continue on to read chapter 18 on your own and
complete the Soul Assignment, but wait to do the Tribe Work
together during your next meeting.)

eighteen

REWRITE YOUR STORY

And suddenly she realized she didn't need an eraser for her past, but a pen to write a beautiful ending.

You've called out your stories and that's half the battle; now it's time to rewrite them. Rewriting and reprogramming is the key to becoming the blissed-out motha you were born to be. Crafting these new stories is just as important as abolishing the old. In fact, it's how you begin to wipe the slate clean. You must create different stories based on how you want to feel. New stories and new programming will ensure that there is no place for the stories of the past to fit into your life. Sometimes when you think you've gotten rid of a story, you find out that it was just away at college or hiking the Andes. You will leave no room for old thoughts, old stories, or old programs by having a plan for when they make a surprise visit and try to move back in. "Sorry, buddy! Mama's remodeled your old bedroom into her new Zen den."

Writing and practicing your new story trains the neurons in your brain to fire a new way. If you feel like garbage every day, it's only because right now your neurons' default is to choose the old easy garbage thoughts. Our brains are not naturally wired to keep us happy; they are wired to be efficient and keep us safe, so if you've been choosing negative thoughts, your brain thinks those are the thoughts you need most often and it will keep those at the forefront for you. Your brain is working on autopilot, traveling down the highway of most frequently used thoughts creating those familiar crappy feelings that come with those familiar crappy thoughts. When you create a new empowering thought and attach it to the positive new feeling, you not only lay down a new superhighway to travel, but by practicing regularly what I am going to teach you, you will create a new memory that stays in the forefront to empower and propel you forward.

The thing you need to know is that, just like taking a new route to a new destination, your brain will feel a bit unsure and lost at first—in fact, the way the brain works is that it's going to want to turn around and go back home to what it knows, even though you fled because "home" was on fire and headed for destruction. It will question whether or not it's making the right choice because it feels foreign, but often (and always for me) the best choice feels challenging at first. It will take time for your brain to choose this new path as your new default, because it's new territory. Give it time (they say about 66 days for a new habit). It takes a little bit to reroute old, habitual traffic and get into new traffic patterns.

The thoughts you have been thinking create how you feel. How you feel is how you see the world. How you see the world is your current reality.

It's not just about saying positive things as I mentioned. You must feel these positive things and allow those feelings to bring you to the desired feeling. We can say stuff all day long, but how you feel walking around during the day is what carries the magnetic pull in the world.

A feeling comes from a thought, and the feeling from the thought is what carries energy. Energy is what you and others around you feel and it's also the thing that you send out into the world to go find more energy that matches it. It's a pretty simple equation: Positive attracts and seeks positive, negative attracts and seeks negative.

The power of thought is never more apparent to me than when I am at the gym or running. Have you ever been in the middle of a run or workout, feeling all is good, when BOOM! A negative thought about something, anything—a worry, a panic, or a bad memory—comes in and it feels like all the wind is taken out of your sails? You literally feel all the energy drain out of you into a puddle around your feet. The run instantly gets harder and the weights get heavier. Next thing you know, you've gone from feeling pretty darn good to feeling ill, tired, or weak—from sixty to zero in the course of a one-second thought. Then the bad feeling follows and you find yourself searching for all of the reasons in your life to feel overwhelmed?

Here's the science of what is actually going on in the brain.

I'll paraphrase how Dr. Joe Dispenza shares how thoughts work in the book *What the Bleep Do We Know!?* The hypothalamus is the portion of the brain that assembles chemicals, called peptides, that match our emotions, which come from our thoughts. There are peptides for every human emotion. The second we experience an emotion, the peptides are released through the bloodstream, where they dock onto one of our cells and send it a signal. A positive thought has a positive chemical release and helps the cells to function properly. A negative thought has a negative chemical release and will start to deplete and damage cells. Prolonged patterns of negative thoughts cause the positive receptors on our cells to lessen, which blocks out vitamins, nutrients, and stops the process of detoxifying our system. If we go by this rule of receiving only more of what we are feeling, then what are you getting more of right now?

Our bodies become addicted to these peptides—both the good and the bad. The emotion and its peptide become our default, the most natural state for us to think, therefore it is actually physically harmful for us to be thinking negative thoughts about our body, our self-image, our job, and other people. On the flip side, telling yourself a positive story and using the techniques of visualization (I'll teach you later on) in order to attract what you do want to feel is one of the most powerful tools you have to be healthy, energetic, powerful, and create a purpose-driven life. Feeling how you want to feel and seeing what you want to see is the secret weapon that Olympian athletes use before any event. I and everyone I admire use this daily, and it works.

AFFIRMATIONS

You may think you know all you need to know about affirmations—except that it's not until you actually create one that fits your specific need and use it properly that they have any power. If you don't already "know" about them, they are one of the best and most consistent ways to change a thought pattern and write a new story in your mind. An affirmation is a statement or sentence used repeatedly to express a statement or belief. Affirmations are important because they will keep you anchored to your new chosen feeling, and feelings create memories. As we switch gears, change direction, and forge a new path, three things usually occur. First, our thoughts regress to the old ways. We start playing those "what if" and "I was fine before," and "wow, this is hard, I can't do this" cards. Second, we future-trip, creating and living out thousands of scenarios that never happen. Third, we start to feel naked without our worry and stress. We gave meaning to our addiction of worry and stress by thinking it's honorable, and if we don't worry, then do we actually care? Will we be in control without it? Affirmations will redirect you to the thoughts you want to think, which will be attached to the feelings you want to feel. The thought is what creates the feeling, but embodying the feeling of what you desire is how you magnetize yourself.

A happy woman is a magnet for her desires.

You can use the power of words to create the positive feelings you desire. When you repeat words and really picture them, what they mean and what it would feel like to embody them, you strengthen the feelings they represent, allowing those feelings to create a new memory to replace the old one.

Whenever an old story or fear comes to visit me, I call it out. I like to say in my head or out loud, "No!" or "Choose again!" then, a prayer from *A Course in Miracles* asking for help to "see it differently." It is always the most comforting reminder that we are not doing this alone. After that I insert my affirmation while focusing on what those life-giving words feel like instead.

A belief is just a thought you keep thinking.
—ABRAHAM HICKS

Affirmations—or what we can think of as our new stories—serve yet another purpose. Not only do they facilitate reprogramming, but an affirmation can quiet your fears and hush the voice of your inner critic. Eventually, as you rewire, you will experience new feelings and positive changes. This may feel a bit whack-a-doo at first, but doing this literally changed my entire life. I still do this and I am always coming up with new affirmations to squash new fears as I continue to grow and evolve into bigger things.

SOUL ASSIGNMENT:

For this Soul Assignment we are going to take that story from the last chapter and create an affirmation so you begin to reprogram your thoughts in order to create a new feeling and outcome. This is where you rewrite your story.

Rewrite the story from the last chapter that you feel is holding you back from creating the life you love.
For this limiting story, come up with a new affirmation

that you will say whenever this old story comes up.
Make sure this affirmation is easy to remember,
realistic for you, and is in "present tense."

Example 1:

Story: "I'm not smart enough and I'm terrified of failing."

Affirmation: "I am enough. As I take the next step, everything will be revealed to me."

Example 2:

Story: "I don't have the time, money, or resources to fulfill my dreams."

Affirmation: "I am resourceful. I seek and attract opportunities that bring me closer to my dreams."

Example 3:

Story: "I'm ashamed of my body and I don't feel worthy."

Affirmation: "I am a beautiful, strong, valuable work in progress."

TRIBE DISCUSSION:

Start out each discussion by sharing what you're grateful for, excited about, and your answers for the questions above. Then, complete the following statement. Remember to respect time and adhere to tribe agreements.

Something else that came up for me was . . .

REMINDER:

Don't forget to set the appointment for your next tribe meeting and choose what chapter or chapters you will discuss next. (Suggestion: Continue on to read chapter 19 on your own and complete the Soul Assignment, but wait to do the Tribe Work together during your next meeting.)

nineteen

GRATITUDE

It is not happy people that are grateful, it's grateful people that are happy.

—UNKNOWN

When my husband and I lived in Minneapolis, we lived near a chain of three lakes. Every day of the year we walked our dog, Waffles, three miles around the lakes. In the spring, the trees filled with beautiful blossoms, ducks and swans would take their time crossing our path with their new babies, and you could smell the promise of summer. It was an indescribable fresh scent that would linger in the air, like molecules of hope and excitement, vibrating through your entire body with every deep breath. In the summer, the shore was lined with the most beautiful wildflowers and everything was painted a vibrant green. The sound of the loons, early in the morning echoing over a perfect glassy lake, is like a song you can't get enough of. Fall at the lakes never ceased to make onlookers grab their chest and gasp. Those moments when the sun lights the trees just right and the colors become iridescent and set the sky ablaze. Each day created a new painting that could only be the masterful work of something that knows exactly what would delight all your senses.

Winter was harsh with subzero temps sometimes for months at a time (brutal, to be honest). I would bundle up, looking like a robber with my face mask and dark, overstuffed, windproof attire, but it was worth it because there were moments when we would walk on the frozen lake and experience something so peaceful. The landscape, covered in white and gray as far as your eyes could see, felt as if for one season the world tucked under a big, fluffy white blanket so it could rest and rejuvenate. Meanwhile, up above, the wind would howl across the lakes, reminding you that it can harden everything in its path. I learned that walking on a frozen lake requires trust, attention, and a bit of stupidity. I totally loved everything about our winter walks. Looking down at the bare spots, that weren't snow covered, you could marvel at the art and sculptures that nature had created in the ice—perfect bubbles, cracks, snowflake-like designs, and leaves and rocks captured for the season in a thick glass case. I was mesmerized by the spots where I could see straight through to the sand. To walk on water and see through it is pretty magnificent.

As picture-perfect as our walks sounded, it took me years to appreciate and see the beauty I just described. I always walked because I needed to, because it was good for the dog, or because I could sneak in some extra exercise and would freak out if I didn't get to move all day. Every step I took was anxious. All

I could think about was what I had to do that day, how over-whelmed I was, and how much I needed to accomplish in order to get to my goals. I became so busy in my head and lived so much in the future that I was not able to experience how won-derful my present was. All I knew was that I was frustrated because I hadn't made it "there" yet. That's all I thought about, and boy did that make me a real ball of fun to be around. And, as we're learning, our thoughts are magnetized. So the more anxious I was, the more things I attracted to be anxious over. I was certain of one thing, however, and that was that I was get-ting zero joy out of my life. I was either living in the past, feeling sick and depressed over what I couldn't change or fix, or I was living in the future never feeling like I was doing enough and never going to be able to achieve what I wanted or get my end-less to-do list done. The "present" was not a place I ever lived. All I could see was what I didn't have yet and that to the world I wasn't enough and didn't have enough, and because of this I was completely blind to what I did have.

My anxiety got so bad on our walks in the morning that my husband finally told me he was fed up and started to call me out. He would say things to me like, "You're so busy in your head, yet you can't do any of those things RIGHT NOW." He would constantly remind me that trying to plan ten steps down the road was robbing me of my happiness and of doing step one. He's a pretty brilliant businessman who has managed hundreds of people at a time, so when he started giving me tips and advice I finally decided to listen. "Time block," as he calls it, so you can work between certain times and then you can plan downtime for yourself to recharge.

Whatever amount of time we delegate for a task, no matter what it is, we will fill it. For example, if you give yourself an hour or four hours to write a blog post, that's how long it will take you to complete the post.

Eventually, I drove him so crazy he started to demand I use this tool. It seems that I had been offered an ultimatum, because basically, my husband wasn't going to walk with me anymore until I stopped being such a "head case." I was treating him (and everyone else in my life) more like an obstacle than someone I chose to do life with. It most often takes someone else calling you out on your crap—like my husband did back then. I can promise you that it never feels good. In fact, to this day, I will normally try to blame anyone else but me for my anxiety. But the hard truth is that it's never anyone else's fault.

If you are depressed you are living in the past. If you are anxious you are living in the future. If you are at peace you are living in the present moment.

—LAO TZU

I wasn't just living in the future on my walks around the lakes, but in most every place in my life. All I could think of was, *I'll be happy when . . .* But the problem with that idea is that upon reaching a goal I would immediately create a new thing I needed in the future that I didn't have right now—a better website, another magazine cover, a book, an event, a program, better friends, more money, a bigger house . . . you know the rest. When you live like this, the future never comes and your actual life does not exist, which means you feel as though you're never living and you're never getting anywhere. This is the formula for anxiety.

In the brief breaks I took from tripping out on the future, I was trudging through my past. My guts were churning as I would replay events in my mind and feel those same terrible feelings again as if it were happening again that very moment. I became a master at making my thoughts feel even worse than the actual event. This is the formula for depression. My present was the past or the future, but it was never where my body was.

The present was being robbed by my made-up timeline. Let's return to the last bit of the quote, the part about peace in the present. "If you are at peace you are living in the present moment." Sounds like a fairy tale, right? I mean, who can really live in the present moment? Well, the truth is that the present moment is the only time that actually exists . . . It's the only place where we have the ability to experience bliss and create our future. You cannot make anything happen in the future or the past. If it's not happening now, don't live there. Live in the now. Your presence IS your power.

Take it easy on yourself though—being present takes practice. It's something that I work to immediately catch and change my thoughts on every single day. I do the work because living in the now is the greatest gift you can give to yourself and to others. It's what it means to live. It's how we access our power to make change. *So how does one get present?*

Trade your expectation for appreciation and the world will change instantly.

—TONY ROBBINS

One word: GRATITUDE. The best and most effective way to live in the moment is through gratitude. Gratitude is not just a practice, it's a way of being. It's the lens I look through to see everything now. Gratitude has the power to remind you you're enough. Gratitude turns what we have into what we want. Every day that we wake up is a good day, and if you do it right, then you will become grateful for even the tough stuff. Maybe not in the moment it's happening, but you'll see what I mean very soon.

I had heard about gratitude having this profound effect on your happiness, but it wasn't until I realized the way I was living was not sustainable anymore that I knew I needed to go all in. It was either that or lose my relationships and kiss any thoughts of inner peace goodbye. I started to play with "choosing" gratitude over anything I was experiencing. I began to ask one of these two questions, "What is this experience or person teaching me?" or "Where is the Bliss in this moment?" Not long after I started this practice, my walk around the lake shifted . . . Had the sounds of the loons always been there? Had the sunlight always sent the beams through the trees like that? Had they always hit the ripples on the lake in that way, causing it to sparkle like a sea of glitter? How had I not noticed that kiss of warmth on my skin, that smell that only the new life of spring could bring before? I felt so . . . overwhelmed, completely stricken with joy. I was finally awake to the beauty that exists in each moment. The question in my mind was no longer about what I needed to do or who I needed to be, but instead it was simply, "What's good?" This also became the question I asked people instead of "How are you?" So I not only changed my perception of my life, I also changed the interactions I was having into more positive ones.

The most insane things started happening the more I practiced this. I realized the answers I was waiting for were right in front of me. What I mean by that is that when you get present, you linger a bit longer in conversations and take sincere interest in people, knowing that there is always magic in whatever moment you are in. When you tap into this, suddenly someone shares some wisdom, gives an answer, or shares a connection that you need. You take time to sit and ponder a question in nature. While enjoying some leisure time, you notice your creativity open up as you see something that sparks an idea you would never have been able to see because of the blinders of stress and upset you had on. I was so self-centered thinking I had to hustle and grind on my own to make things happen. Little did I realize my lack of presence was keeping me from the blessings, people, and interactions life was trying to offer me. I was too busy and too stressed to receive the blessings that were waiting for me.

As I sit and write about my years at the lakes, tears roll down my face. I am still so darn grateful for the realization that I get to be on this planet. I get to live fully in each moment. I am keenly aware of all that I would be missing out on if I didn't stay present. Life is full of beauty and joy and peace, but it would be hard to access any of it without deep gratitude. Without my lens of gratitude, I had spent years living a joyless, anxious, and rather ungrateful life.

I will never do that again. Wrapping my hands around my coffee cup this morning, feeling how perfect the shape is while it warms my hands, reminds me how much I love me a good mug. Holding it up to my mouth, I take in the smell, I mean really take it in—thinking about the aroma, wondering where the beans came from and who took the care and time to pick them. I grab the vintage-looking, glass mason jar with a tin lid, which reminds me of my grandmother and her years of making strawberry preserves. It's full of almond milk from my fridge (that kept it cold overnight—thank you, fridge!), the milk that my friend Jackie made for me. I observe the creamy beige color with flecks of spices floating in it. I use my milk frother, which forms lovely foam on top of my coffee. I bring this perfect mug up to my mouth, feeling the texture of froth on my lips. With my first sip, my tastebuds light up and I feel all the love that I brought in with each thought and memory. The care given to the beans, the milk, the mug, and the memories of my grandmother. Now that's a good morning.

It takes me only five minutes to make coffee, but I am so overwhelmed with gratitude that:

> *I get to drink really good coffee.*
> *I have this mug I'm obsessed with.*
> *I have a friend who cares enough to make me really*
>   *yummy almond milk.*
> *I have a milk frother.*
> *I have electricity, for Pete's sake!*

Clearly, I could go on and on about my coffee. This particular morning I was in such a state of gratitude that I never, not once, thought about all my afternoon appointments. This is an example of how intensely effective my gratitude practice has become.

It is the way I see everything. I know this sounds crazy, but when you get good at this, you get really good. Someone can flip me off in the car, and while my blood still boils for a few seconds, I can say thank you for letting me practice my patience and empathy on them. I will take a minute to realize that they are not present and they are probably having a rough day, are in a hurry, and can't see past their stress. Sometimes, if I remember, I say a quick prayer for them to someday be able to slow down and experience what I am able to. I have even started to fall in love with my workouts because I am so grateful that I have a body that moves and carries me through this life. Sound too good to be true? I thought so, too, but it's not. Deep gratitude can be yours with practice.

The simple act of being grateful creates feelings of gratitude. The feeling of gratitude will magnetize your life and attract more in which to be grateful. It's a snowball effect. Each emotion you feel brings more of that same feeling, and each feeling will bring more of what caused that emotion. The key to this is learning to feel grateful even when you are not feeling grateful—to feel gratitude when gratitude is not our default feeling. Maybe you're in a rough patch and are having trouble seeing what could make you feel grateful for anything. Oftentimes, when we are having trouble, it's because we are focusing our thoughts and energy on what we are lacking or what we are not enjoying. However, do you notice how focusing on what you don't have will only create more lack and feelings of lack? Getting into a state of gratitude calls for nothing more than a shift in focus, so let's do that now. I'll help you get started. It's as easy as making a list. Make a list of at least twenty things that you can think of that makes you grateful. Big, small, it doesn't matter. Just start writing things

down. In fact, I'll share a short version of my list to get you
started.

my relationship with God
my husband
my Goldendoodle, Waffles
family
humor
a functioning body
surfing in the ocean
clothing—especially cute clothes
champagne
appliances
free self-expression
the movies
healthy food
dark chocolate
almond milk lattes
sunshine and rain
a lovely home
music
dancing
a cozy bed and nice sheets
coffee
technology
books
sunsets
spray tans

kombucha
charcuterie plates
crystals
moonlight
snowboarding
(my list is endless . . .)

Eventually your list will get very detailed and also very personal. That's the point. It's your life. What are *you* grateful for?

Keep in mind, the goal of this list is not only to keep adding more to it and getting more detailed, but to reflect on it every day. You can do this first thing in the morning—with your cup of coffee like me. Whenever you eat anything, use anything, or go anywhere, try thinking of the people who made those things, planted the seeds, built the structures, etc. How much love and time went into creating that moment for you? Everything will become a gift when you take a moment to savor each thing and simply say thank you.

This is now your magical tool to get present and put things in perspective. Remember this—gratitude supercharges your manifestation. It is the feeling that attracts more to be grateful for.

Are you ready to make your list of twenty?

SOUL ASSIGNMENT:

Create your list of twenty things you are grateful for and post them in a place where you can reflect on them daily.

TRIBE DISCUSSION:

Start by sharing what you're grateful for, excited about, your list, what you experienced while writing it, and what your new gratitude practice will be daily. Then, complete the statement below. Remember to respect time and adhere to tribe agreements.

Something else that came up for me was . . .

REMINDER:

Don't forget to set the appointment for your next tribe meeting and choose what chapter or chapters you will discuss next. (Suggestion: Continue on to read chapter 20 on your own and complete the Soul Assignment, but wait to do the Tribe Work together during your next meeting.)

twenty

CREATING YOUR ENERGY HABITS

When people tell me they have no motivation, no clarity, a spiritual disconnection, and/or anxiety, I know they have an energy problem. It's not that you don't have energy, you're born with it—it's that you're somehow blocking the incoming energy and leaking your own.

Why am I talking about energy? Because when you have no energy you have no passion, connection, excitement, action, enthusiasm, movement, happiness, or vitality. You have no willpower to create a change, let alone follow your bliss. Lack of energy means you're tired and tired means you feel like an irritable, carb-crazed psychopath—or is that just me? I need a nap. Did you just say crackers?

You're going to need all the energy and willpower you can access to go to the next level. So let's figure out where to get more of it from, shall we?

Where does energy come from? If your answer is food and sleep, you're partially right, but I'm certainly not running any marathons after a buffet, or doing anything of value, for that matter. Most likely when I eat too much "energy," all I've got energy for is unbuttoning my pants and watching a documentary on sloths. I've also slept so much out of boredom or feeling depressed that it actually made me even more tired.

So let's reassess. Since God is the Source of all energy and we are actually made up of energy, and everything around us is made up of energy, my inner Columbo says the best place to start would be looking at what is blocking us from feeling what is already ours. Energy, willpower, and connection to God are natural things if we have the discipline around the habits that support them. So let's take a look at the fastest ways we can access more energy.

WITHOUT ENERGY YOU HAVE NO WILLPOWER TO CHANGE

There seem to be these mythical creatures that walk among us with otherworldly abilities to say no to all the tantalizing shit that all of us normal folk can't seem to resist.

"Holy balls! Are you trying to tell me Taco Bell just wrapped a taco inside a burrito, inside a quesadilla, and for a limited time? I can't say no to that!" *Ugh!* "How will I ever get my summer bod if I can't stop running to the border?"

Hey, I get it—this was me for years. I wasn't ready to miss out or see what it really took to get that better body and abundant mindset. I wasn't yet in enough pain—my comfort zone wasn't uncomfortable enough. Before now, we weren't ready to know what it takes to change. We choose to look away when the "lucky ones" go for that three-mile run every day, even when they're tired or when they go out and have a salad and sashimi, even when they want the giant dirty-sushi sailboat all for themselves.

But now you're ready to learn what goes on behind the scenes so you can access the same secret strength that they tap into daily. Willpower is not just gifted to the special few. It's true, we all have the ability to access it, to increase it, and to use it to help us reach our goals.

HOW IT WORKS

I'll paraphrase what positive psychology researcher Shawn Achor shares in his book *The Happiness Advantage*: Willpower is like a muscle, and it lives in the part of the brain called the prefrontal cortex. It is important to know that we are not born with a set amount of willpower; however, we are able to build willpower in the same way we're able to build muscle.

Picture willpower as a glass of water. When you wake up each day, the glass is already half empty because you didn't eat well, think well, or didn't sleep much the night before, and as you go throughout your day, each choice you make and task you do consumes some of that water. If you are not in tune with how to live in order to contain it, you will end up leaking all of it by the late afternoon, which is the reason most people make the worst choices from seven to twelve at night. You just have nothing left because you started without enough to make it through the day.

The more choices you make outside of your habits and outside of what's familiar, the more energy is used, therefore draining your willpower. Think of it this way . . . how much effort (mental or physical) does it take to brush your teeth, get dressed, drink water, drive to work, hug your best friend, or walk your dog? If that is routine for you—*not that much, right?* But every time we have to go outside of our normal routine for a decision or new action that takes a lot of thought, restraint, and effort, we use up a large part of our supply for that day. That is why we need to focus on just one or two (one is better) small changes at a time until they become a habit. This is also why all or nothing never ever works!

You can dramatically increase your energy and willpower supply with the following routine I share in this chapter. Not only will you feel happier and more energized but it will seem easier to follow through on your goals.

CREATE YOUR ENERGY ROUTINE

Now it's time to create a routine that not only supports your healthy mindset but also supports that beautiful body of yours that carries you through your life.

Habit 1: Get a Good Night's Sleep

Fact: People who don't get enough sleep suffer from mild prefrontal dysfunction, which is recognizable to many as "sleep deprivation," which can lead to food cravings and poor decision-making. When you're exhausted, you don't have the (will)power to make good choices, and life gets pretty stressful. Stress, in turn, causes the release of cortisol, a hormone that increases appetite and hinders your body's ability to burn fat easily. Ever noticed how people who don't sleep enough find it super challenging to lose weight? It's no coincidence. When you don't get the proper amount of sleep (reach REM stage), the body doesn't produce its own appetite suppressant called leptin, which curbs cravings. The next day not only are we exhausted and willpowerless, but we're hungry.

Personally, I know that sleep is singlehandedly my biggest game changer. I am a completely different person when I sleep less than eight hours (this time will vary for each individual). The only thing I can focus on is how exhausted I am—and carbs. My only thoughts are about rolling like thunder under the covers with crackers and making love to some pasta, pizza, and champagne. Sorry, that's my no-sleep, red-room fantasy, and it's one that is guaranteed to leave me less than satisfied. I have learned that I have to say goodnight and goodbye early. Otherwise, the world gets a cranky B walking around all crazy like, "Unless your name is Ben or Jerry, get the F outta my face." Not cute— I know you feel me.

I suggest setting your alarm for bed (I know it sounds a little bass-ackwards, but hear me out). If you're not already doing this, set an alarm on your phone that tells you to get prepped for the next day and get into bed. Once you hear it, you know that it's time to get your butt to bed, because you're creating a habit that can shift your life and change your body. Start with twenty-minute increments and work backward until you are in bed at the time you desire. If you normally crawl under the covers around midnight and you are aiming for 10:30, then start by setting your alarm for around 11:30 to begin getting ready to crawl in bed. Yes, you may read or just lie there staring at the ceiling, but this is only your body adjusting to getting in bed earlier. Don't watch TV or get out your phone. The light used in the screens keeps your mind awake. Remember, this is proven to help change your mood and your health. What could you accomplish if you felt awesome everyday? Now go to bed!

Habit 2: Move It

My friend Jim Kwik, who is a brain expert, says, "The mind grooves when the body moves." In fact, when you don't move, your body and mind are not functioning properly. Moving is a part of us; it's built in to who we are. If we take a trip back in time, we were made to spend the day gathering food; water; dancing around fire; hunting; building shelter; cooking; taking care of babies, elderly, tribes; washing clothes; making clothes; and so much more. We didn't have time to sit. Heck, we didn't have time to be depressed! There was too much to do just to survive. Modern conveniences have created a plethora of modern problems that we never even thought would be problems! Our comforts are literally killing us. We now know that a sedentary life is worse on your health than smoking a pack of cigarettes a day.

I can pinpoint my success to the things I share in this book, but I believe the start of my spiritual awakening came from exercise. Initially I started exercising due to teasing because I was chubbier than my friends, and later on in life it was something as simple as walking that saved me.

In 2008, my husband, Chris, got laid off from his job in the banking and finance world. We were young, stupid, and over-extended. My husband was super successful at a young age and we were constantly moving from city to city. With moving up the ladder there always came another location. We thought the money and the big raises would last forever, so we invested in bigger and better homes with each move (our third new home together in just a few years). When the financial crash happened we lost our home, our cars, and our way. Because he was the primary breadwinner at the time this meant we lost everything. The two things we had were each other and our walks. We moved into a tiny one-bedroom condo and we walked every day together, sometimes for hours until we moved through the pain and fear into an answer. We prayed and asked what we should do and then we just waited. Some days on our walks we heard nothing, but we felt peace, on others we laughed, screamed, and jumped with thoughts and ideas of a better way, and eventually these walks had us leaning into the possibility that perhaps this was the best thing to ever happen to us . . . This positive thought around a negative situation was the beginning of our new plan and new life. We walked until we found the solutions we were looking for. In fact, we tell people this is one of the biggest marriage tips out there for being happy—to go move together daily. Whenever an argument, problem, or question we can't answer arises, we say "Take *it* on a walk!" Shacked up or single, go move that bod. Add listening to podcasts (try EarnYourHappy.com) or audiobooks on the walks and your life will be changed!

Moving is not just about looking good, although that may be your original catalyst, but it's about connecting to whom you are and making your way through the feelings that can consume us if we stay stagnant. My friend Rosie, who is a yoga and meditation teacher to famous athletes and celebs, says "the issues are in our tissues," meaning that our problems and emotional traumas get stuck in our bodies. Not only is it important to deal with them emotionally, but we also have to find ways to physically move that stuck energy through our body. We need our body far more than it needs us. Find a way that you LIKE moving and keep showing up. When that gets boring, try a new way, but just don't stop moving.

Habit 3: Morning Mantra, Meditation, Visualization

Morning Mantra

A mantra is like having antivirus software constantly keeping you safe. You wake up to messages about what tried to attack you overnight and what is currently trying to scramble your files. Your mantra is your software that keeps you clear and is constantly cleaning up those thoughts that are trying to take you down.

Again, I'm pretty basic, so I like to keep it simple. Because I love sleep and I don't love waking up, my morning mantra reminds me exactly how I desire to feel and view my life . . . oh, and also not to be a crabby a-hole. Try making a one- to two-sentence statement that you recite first thing in the morning when your eyes open. Just do it—no matter how weird it feels.

Oh, and I would never teach you some bologna that didn't actually change my life in a massive way.

Here are some goodies:

> » *I'm happier, healthier, wealthier, and more fit than I was yesterday.*
> » *Life is fun and easy, and there is plenty of time for everything! (My current mantra)*
> » *I am a perfect, beautiful work in progress and I'm uncovering more things I love about myself each day.*
> » *I am abundant, healthy, and grateful for all I get to do today.*
> » *I am powerful and connected to the divine. I am supported and everything on my path is here to help me grow.*

Now, write it on some Post-it notes, set your alarm on your phone, and put this reminder in there so it's the first thing you see, or get it tattooed on your forehead. Either will work.

Meditation

First off, there is no wrong way. So if you're saying things like, "I can't meditate, I don't like it; meditating is for stinky hippies; I can't focus; I'm too stressed or I don't have time," then you're probably too busy thinking someone else's thoughts. And here's why that's a problem . . .

We seem to be turning into a bunch of programmed robots

who are more familiar with checking out of our brains and bodies and checking into what the people think on our devices. We are more addicted to the dopamine hits we get off checking for "likes" than we are with checking in with what makes us happy and brings fulfillment. I was just at a business mastermind event where an insider from a popular app came to speak to a tiny group of us. He let us know that they are spending millions of dollars on research figuring out how to get us even more addicted to our devices. Still think you're thinking for yourself? Meditation because . . . THAT.

But don't stress over something that is meant to de-stress you. You can literally feel some pretty mind-blowing effects from just five minutes a day in the most unsuspecting places. One thing I want to be clear on is that meditation can take many different forms and is NOT the emptying of one's mind. Instead, it is the art of choosing what stays and what goes. Let's focus more on slowing it down and infusing it with loving thoughts.

Here's what meditation really looks like.

Before meditation:

Nooo! I hate that alarm. Did I even sleep? Fuck I'm tired. I want a doughnut. Why am I so fat? I hate my body. What's for lunch? I feel like shit from last night's dinner. Why do I do that to myself? I'm such a loser. God, I can't put on jeans today, please don't make me. I need coffee. I'll never get my to-do list done. I hate this fucking job. I am so stuck. Why didn't he call me back? I might as well go adopt my forty-seven cats now. What if

*I just run away . . . yes, to an island far away from it all.
I just want to sleep forever. Why can't I feel this tired at
night? Whyyyyyyy . . .*

During meditation:

*I'm so tired. No . . . I'm here. I'm breathing. I'm wasting
time. Let go, let go, let go. This feels good. Breath. This
is pointless. I'm choosing peace. Let go . . . Awwwww,
breath. What am I grateful for? How could I be of service
to someone today? I could smile more. God I don't want
to call my mom, she's so negative. What is this actually
doing? No. Choose again. I'm so grateful I have a mom
to call. Breathe, let go, reframe. I choose love . . . How
do I want to feel today? What would I be thinking if I
wanted to feel good? But I feel tired. Let go, how do I
want to feel? What am I grateful for? Breathe . . . Let go,
let go, let go. Choose again. I'm so grateful to be alive,
have a job, have friends, and have choices . . . ahhh . . .
Wait, was that, like, a moment of peace? That was trippy!
Craaaapppp!!! I lost it.*

Welcome to day one and once in a while day ninety-one.
Glamorous, huh? It's like teaching a toddler how to sit still in a
toy store. Don't worry, in time your inner toddler learns to focus
and find peace for longer periods of time and actually begins to
impress you with their discernment, ability to communicate their
real feelings, and self-restraint in order to wait and choose the
actions that create the outcomes they desire.

I'm going to give you a little more motivation on some of the other reasons you should give it a go. Meditation is about the long term. It helps you slow the behavior of chasing the dopamine habits and going for the practices that create that long-term feel-good serotonin. It also helps reduce anxiety (in kids too!), stress, blood pressure, and headaches. It can also help increase creativity, productivity, and positive thoughts.

Here's a simple practice Chris and I do most mornings. Set a timer for five to ten minutes. Start with a one-minute (or whatever you want) prayer of thanks and gratitude. It doesn't have to be elaborate, just say what's on your mind even if all you can say is "Dear God, thank you for my coffee." I like to get grateful for my loved ones, my health, and my to-do list. Next, depending on if you desire to feel more calm or if you're looking for answers, you can do one of these.

If you want answers or guidance, try this prayer from *A Course in Miracles*:

What would you have me do, where would you have me go, what would you have me say and to whom?

If you feel anxious, try this. This is one of my favorite meditations that helps me get present quickly.

Sense-drenching meditation. Set a timer for five minutes, close your eyes, sit comfortably, and bring your focus to taking long deep inhales and exhales for five breaths. Next it's time to drench the senses, aka focus on each one and what it's telling you. Take about one minute or less for each and really get into it. Get as focused and detailed as possible.

Sight: What are you seeing—yes, I know your eyes are closed, but you're still seeing something (squiggles, black, colors, visions, what?).

Hearing: What are you hearing right now? Maybe the hum of the air conditioner, light music, your breath, the breeze, your heartbeat? What?

Smell: Take it in, try to name everything you can in the air.

Taste: What does your mouth taste like? Can you taste the air? Your breakfast, toothpaste, what? If it tastes like nothing, think about what nothing tastes like.

Touch: What are you feeling? What is supporting you? What does your clothing feel like? How does your skin feel? Is the earth supporting you? Does gravity feel good right now? Explain to yourself what your body is feeling.

Visualization

This is how I've received my biggest and best ideas and how I've been able to be ready for them when they manifest. These are Wonder Woman-, Beyoncé-, and Oprah-type skills. If you really take this serious, you will become a manifesting machine. Your new superhero name will become Wonder-Bey-Rah—manifester of the miraculous.

Visualization is the dress rehearsal for your dream future. Your body can't tell the difference between what you envision and what is real. Let me take you through a perfectly awkward exercise. All you have to do is visualize and get really detailed thinking about a hot, steamy moment with The Rock and a squeezie bottle of chocolate sauce (or your food of choice) to get the body primed for sexy time. Now observe how you feel when you picture the same thing with Richard Simmons and a caulking gun full of some hot liver pâté. Two opposite visions, yes? Isn't visualization powerful?

You don't have to do a thing but get good at thinking about the thing you desire for your body to get ready, comfortable, and familiar with what you want it to do. This is just like your goals (time to stop thinking about The Rock, unless of course he's your end goal). Get good at seeing yourself accomplishing them and focus on feeling the feeling that comes from the thought. That emotion is what produces the memory in your body and thoughts, and it's sending out the same chemical reactions that the actual experience will create. Hence why we can also get nervous just thinking about jumping out of an airplane or doing some other thing that scares us.

The main factor of being successful is the ability to see yourself succeeding. This can be achieved through regular visualization. Your mind is a problem-solving machine. When you give it something to focus and work on through regular visualization, it goes to work trying to solve that puzzle and creates ideas to reach your goal long after the visualization is over.

Visualization ties an emotional response to your goals when you make sure to focus on the feelings that the vision is creating. It makes them so real that you can't imagine not following through, and can even begin to feel as if you already have. Researchers say that one hour of visualization is equal to seven hours of physical practice. Again, you get what you focus on. I realize I'm repeating myself, but it's only so you're able to see that what you've been thinking and picturing is what you've been feeling—and feelings are the magnet for all you've been experiencing! This is why it is imperative that you learn how to properly and effectively use this magic by only choosing to focus on and visualize what you desire and are grateful for—or you will keep getting more of what you don't want!

I can attest firsthand to the power of visualization. When I injured myself before a competitive fitness/dance routine a few years ago, I was not physically able to run through it each day in order to learn it on time. I was convinced I would have to back out of the competition due to my injury. I called a friend who was a gymnast, and she let me in on the secret of visualization. Athletes are injured so often (or need down time) that they have to practice this in order to be ready for the big day or game. After two weeks with no practice and just twenty minutes of visualization a day, I came back stronger than ever and had memorized the routine like the back of my hand without ever actually physically doing it. Olympians and professional sports teams have been using this as a regular part of their practice too.

I also use this before every speaking event I have ever done. A week to two weeks out I picture how I want to feel onstage and how I want my audience to feel. I see myself channeling a loving message and powerfully delivering it until I can really feel the experience and memorize it in my body.

How to do it:

I like to tack on visualization to the end of my meditation. I always say, "Do whatever you are most likely to stick to." So if you need to, just try doing three to five minutes of each or throw on a song that elevates your mood and use that as your timer. Get present, meditate first, and then do a visualization. Even that small amount will make a huge difference in a few weeks! If you can do longer, awesome!

Start picturing what your ideal day is. Picture yourself at your goal. Let yourself really feel what it feels like to be there, in it. What are you seeing, smelling, feeling, hearing, and saying, what are you wearing, where are you, who is around you, what are they saying, how does it feel to accomplish it, and how proud are the people around you? Once you become good at this (and you will in time), make sure that when you're visualizing, you're stepping into your body and actually looking out through your own eyes—not just seeing yourself as an outsider doing the actions. This will also take practice, but eventually you will master it.

The most important thing here is to feel yourself living your day and events with ease and to feel deep gratitude, happiness, and joy around whatever you're visualizing. Feelings are the highest level of attraction, so if you're vibrating on the frequency of your goals and the life you desire most of the time, that's what you will be calling into your life.

Now that we understand the importance of energy, I want to add one more layer to that. And that's your physical body—that gorgeous vessel that houses your soul. Take care of that and your whole life just feels easier. From what you eat to moving your body on a regular basis, let's dive a little deeper into some practices that assist you in reaching your bliss even faster.

Habit 4: Food

You are what you eat, don't be fast, cheap, or fake.
                                                        —UNKNOWN

When you're full of toxic shit, nothing flows—mentally and physically. If you're living a "clogged" life, you're most likely backed up and creating messes at really inconvenient times.

I realized I was trying to fill a spiritual void and a pit of exhaustion and boredom with food and I was trying to numb my anxiety, stress, and fear with alcohol. Instead of really looking at the root of the issues, I kept swallowing the quick fixes and hoping I could wash it all away with some temporary pleasures. But the more I stuffed in, the more the pit expanded.

It wasn't until I realized I couldn't hate myself thin, sabotage myself into success, and abuse myself into self-love that I was forced to try another way, a way that seemed completely counterintuitive to me. It wasn't until I started to forgive myself quickly, and comfort and support myself through thoughts and self-talk, that I finally got a glimpse of what it means to really like being in my own skin. I had to think and fuel myself like someone who already loved herself, before I actually did. See, love is a verb so it can only come after you have acted in a loving way. You must do these things for yourself in order to experience a true loving relationship with yourself and your body.

Food is one of THE biggest blocks I have encountered for myself. My ten-plus years in the health field have shown me that it's a block for a large chunk of the population as well. If we were really just talking about food here, we would all just learn the science of nutrition and follow that. But it's not a food problem, it's a self-love problem. We use and view food as just about everything except as an energy-rich gift to fuel us through our life.

Since I'm a well-versed food-user/abuser, I'll begin. I have used food as a reward, a loyal friend, entertainment, a crutch, a punishment, a mind-numbing drug, a pillow (c'mon, I can't be the only one who's passed out on a pizza), and so much more. I have been addicted to it, repulsed by it, and scared of it. I have cried over it, panicked over it, and felt imprisoned by it. Of course, you can still be spiritual, successful, and happy if you don't eat awesomely, but life will always have a slight filter over it. You may not even realize the crispness and focus you're missing out on until you start making higher-vibe food choices. I hear people say, "I had no idea I could feel this good!" all the time. I also hear people say they have massive clarity around their purpose, goals, or life when they start eating high-vibe—aka healthy shiz. In case you're wondering, you can't pop open a can of high vibes . . .

Rule of thumb: Want to feel connected to God? Eat food from the earth. Wanna feel connected to scary clowns named Ronald? Eat fast food. Capisce?

Put one hand on your belly and the other on your heart while you read this paragraph—what does your body feel like or say to you when I say this . . . Eat from the earth, eat with appreciation, eat beautiful, colorful, fresh, diverse, natural foods made with love, eat slowly, eat for energy, chew and savor each flavor, eat with how you want to feel in mind, eat for fueling all of your desires, relationships, and dreams. Does your body say yes? Does it have an idea of what will make it perform better for you? Do you know what would help you unleash that healthy, vital goddess who's just waiting to bust out? I think you do. Ask again and write down your first answers. Get crystal clear on how you want to feel and ask yourself before you order, eat, or check out at the grocer "How is this food going to make me feel?"—the more you do this, the more you will be eating from your very own intuition.

This will take a bit of practice, but if you feel lost, instead of labeling yourself, taking anything away, or thinking things are off-limits, start by allowing yourself to eat ANYTHING and ANY amount you want as long as it's natural, as fresh as possible, and from the earth. Look at each choice and ask how it will make you feel. What emotion does it feed and nurture? The more we bring our awareness to our food the more we will know what to eat to feel the way we want to feel.

Trial and error are your best friends here and your body won't lie. It will always give you feedback through your feelings, mood, and energy.

Try this: While you eat this healthy food, picture your eyes, skin, organs, heart, muscles, kidneys, liver, colon, and brain all rejoicing and saying THANK YOU for this gift of fuel that they can finally use to help you with whatever you need. Your body wants to be your ally, but you must first give it what it needs to go to work for you!

Eventually the goal is to shake out at about 80 percent as healthy as possible for the day. While it may take a bit to reach that goal, it's an amazing thing to aim for!

The only difference between where you are now and where you want to go is how well you know yourself and what you are willing to settle for. Women who have the food thing "figured out" have gone through an intense self-examination process. Once they feel the impact that eating can have on their entire lives, they don't settle for anything other than what makes them feel their best. They are acutely aware that their choices make or break their emotions, relationships, and energy. Yes, I said relationships. How you feel all-around is reflected in everything. Low-level emotions, choices, and energy attract low-level people, and outcomes. It's about constantly weighing the outcomes of the choices at hand and choosing the one that ends in the highest level of happiness and fulfillment—even if that's the least appealing choice in the moment. It's all about learning to live for the endgame the majority of the time. This will require a complete flip-flop in thinking and will take some time. You will spend less time in brief, instant gratification but more time in complete bliss and fulfillment. I need your trust on this one—but it's a promise.

Oh, and in case you're thinking it, you're not broken. I've never met a willing, committed person who didn't eventually figure things out. Source saw you as beyond worthy and loved you enough to gift you that beating heart of yours. It's up to you to stop settling and start choosing to see yourself and your life as a miracle. Until you choose you, and I mean really *choose* to give yourself a fighting chance, no one else will.

You are a work in progress and the journey is where you learn the most about yourself. From a girl whose favorite game used to be "Edward Forty Hands" (duct-tape a 40-ounce beer to each hand until they're gone), I promise that what you view as joy now can and will drastically change if you want it to.

SOUL ASSIGNMENT:

From the Energy Routines shared in this chapter, pick the most pressing habit that will make the biggest impact in your life right now. Remembering how willpower works, only focus on one habit at a time.

> *What habit will you focus on first, and how will you schedule it in?*

TRIBE DISCUSSION:

Start by sharing what you're grateful for, excited about, and which habit you chose to focus on first. Then, complete the statements below. Remember to respect time and adhere to tribe agreements.

> *The action I am taking and scheduling into my calendar each week toward my new habit is . . .*

*I would like to be held accountable to my new habit
each week by . . .*
Something else that came up for me was . . .

REMINDER:

Don't forget to set the appointment for your next tribe meeting and choose what chapter or chapters you will discuss next.
(Suggestion: Continue on to read chapter 21 on your own and
complete the Soul Assignment, but wait to do the Tribe Work
together during your next meeting.)

twenty-one

RESISTANCE TRAINING & YOUR PURPOSE

Rule of thumb: The more important a call or action is to our soul's evolution, the more resistance we will feel toward pursuing it.

—STEVEN PRESSFIELD

RESISTANCE AND YOUR PURPOSE

First let's talk purpose. I don't believe purpose is this thing that hits you like a lightning bolt and suddenly you know you're supposed to be a chef, open a restaurant, and go for a Michelin star. For some this may be the case, but for most, myself included, I had to experience a lot of resistance before I knew what it was. It doesn't make you more or less special if you do or don't feel your purpose, or feel the call to change the world, for that matter. I do believe, however, that our purpose is to wake up each day and create one. Of course, it's even better if you can create one around the things that bring you joy. Ultimately, our purpose is just to share love, enjoy ourselves, and follow our bliss, but we're so out of touch with what we actually enjoy that we first have to get back in touch with this feeling.

I was on a long walk last night because I needed to clear my head and I thought about the phrase "Enjoy yourself." It literally means to enjoy who you are in an experience—not the experience or thing itself. I mean, how crazy to really think that enjoying who you are is the whole purpose! God made you and wants you to enjoy the vessel in which you experience Him and His creations through. How simple, right? When you enjoy yourself, you're enjoying God's gifts. So what if we started asking ourselves the following questions: What are we doing and who are we around when we enjoy how we feel and who we are showing up as? After all, they say the reason we fall in love with people is because we enjoy how they make us feel—aka we enjoy the experience of who we are around them. Find those things, create reasons to do them often, and therefore you have revealed parts of your purpose.

I realize now that I enjoy myself and feel most connected to God when I'm learning, moving my body, and teaching what I learned. I took this feeling of joy and connection as a hint to what I should build my purpose around. I knew I wanted to experience feeling this connection to Source more often, and I also knew I wanted a way to feel valuable and add value to others while doing the things I loved. With all this information, in time I pieced together a life doing what I enjoy the most and I became a speaker, author, teacher, fitness trainer, and a forever student.

Resistance Has a Message for You

Now on to resistance. You must believe that all the resistance you feel is happening for you. Think about it. Without resistance training, aka strength training and weights, we can't get stronger in the gym. The key is understanding how to use the resistance. You would never lie down and pile weights on your body so they crush you, right? No, you would take those same crushing weights and you would figure out how to use them to your advantage to help you gain the strength. Then you would keep working through the resistance until you got the result you wanted. The most interesting part of all is that in order to increase your results once you've reached your goal, you must increase the amount of resistance.

Unfortunately, most people quit before the resistance, pain, or obstacle gives us the strength and lessons we needed to advance to the next level.

I work with thousands of women, many who are riding the Cray-Hound Bus down "OMG I Need a Change Lane." (I know it's a long name for a street, but it's a long road.) But like most of us who decide to travel from our head to our heart or from our resistance to our purpose, it takes some road blocks and obstacles to finally get us to "detour in the right direction" as Gabrielle Bernstein says.

× × ×

Resistance is a brilliant and punctual shape-shifter.

The very second you make the decision, set the goal, announce to the world, or put yourself out there, resistance is coming for you. Now hold on, before you slip into that full-on panic attack and picture your life going up in flames, I said it's coming *for you*, but not in a way that it's actually trying to take you down. But it is in fact coming *for you*—to help you solidify that the choices you made are the ones you need for your soul's evolution. I didn't say it brings you what you expect, but it will deliver the tests to make sure this is what you want and that you're ready.

It's not here to watch you fail. It's actually here for you to practice pushing against so you can build the strength you need down the road. A good trainer and teacher pushes you past your perceived failure in order to show you things you didn't believe you were capable of doing. Obstacles and fear are your *resistance* training and they're happening for you. Thank resistance when it appears; it's telling you you're ready and exactly where you need to be. It's only when you reject it and its message that you reject your own purpose and path.

Resistance is your know-it-all friend that says, "I told you so." It's your coworker that asks if you're doing "that healthy thing again?" It's your family and friends that don't understand your lifestyle. It's the guilt you feel about taking an hour to exercise when you have children. It's your spouse that gives you an eye roll when you say you're going to try something new. It's the money you need but don't yet have for that new business. It's the voice in your head that says they're right and you're wrong, that tells you you're just not enough—not strong enough, not smart enough, not bold enough, not pretty enough. Resistance can be a total D-bag.

No matter who you are, it's guaranteed that on this journey resistance will show up for you. The faster it shows up, the more you know you have big things in the world you are meant to do.

Do you recognize any of these forms of resistance?

Lack of purpose
Too busy
Procrastination
Kids
Losing friends
No support
Money
The weather
Family
Work obligations
Exhaustion
Religious beliefs
Health
Fear
Drama
Depression

Food

Alcohol

Boredom

Excessive education, events, or courses

I could keep the list going, but are you ready for the truth? Good, because the truth is that resistance is the only thing that will help us change. The presence of resistance is not negative, it's normal. It's a part of life. It, too, has a purpose—to remind us to keep moving, keep redirecting, keep forging ahead, keep feasting on the beauty that is life, and to keep us connecting, growing, and contributing. We want to be on the same road as resistance because resistance is how we get stronger and know we are on our path to purpose.

So what have you been resisting? Or the better question is, *where are you not taking action?* Often, you will find the answer somewhere hidden, somewhere that seems innocent. Like the second cup of coffee in the morning. You get that feeling of bittersweet enjoyment, because it's so good sitting a bit longer, yet so bad because that tiny pleasure is keeping you from the real satisfaction of time spent on pursuing your goal, passion, or purpose. Or maybe you've been on this journey for a long time and instead of taking that next big leap, you go to another seminar, read another book, do another competition, or run another marathon because you're good at it. This is a sneaky and slow departure from our purpose; we end up paying with our potential being unmet at the end of our lives.

Purpose-driven aligned action will immediately cure the pain of resistance and lost time, and the good news is that it's never too late to begin.

For now, let's do some major reframing of resistance when it comes up. In order to do so, we must study—as a neutral observer—our lives to find out where resistance comes up.

SOUL ASSIGNMENT:

Focus on your day—just one day a time. Ask yourself the following five questions, which will help shed light on where resistance shows up. Take time and answer each question. You might be surprised at what you discover.

> *Where is resistance showing up the most for you right now?*
> *What form does it take?*
> *What is the message you think it's trying to give you?*
> *How could this be here to make you stronger?*
> *How will you use it and move through it?*

TRIBE DISCUSSION:

Start out each discussion by sharing what you're grateful for, excited about, and your answers for the questions above. Then, complete the statement below if there is time. Remember to respect time and adhere to tribe agreements.

> *Something else that came up for me during this*
> *exercise was . . .*

REMINDER:

Don't forget to set the appointment for your next tribe meeting and choose what chapter or chapters you will discuss next. (Suggestion: Continue on to read chapter 22 on your own and complete the Soul Assignment, but wait to do the Tribe Work together during your next meeting.)

twenty-two

A MESSAGE FROM YOUR SOUL

There is a reason it's taken a while for you to let me out. Trust you've not lost or wasted any time, as now has always been my expected time of arrival. Your procrastination holds sacred messages for you and has allowed the unnecessary to fall away to make room for what brings you life. Each moment has been preparing you for my emergence—because, darling, you know I only make big entrances. You just needed some extra challenges to practice on so you don't dim us when people say we are too bright—this is when you know your light has stretched far beyond the shadows. It won't be easy and it's okay to be scared. You can find comfort in knowing you are connected to and protected by the ultimate source of power. Have faith. I take no shortcuts, I don't coddle, and I don't apologize for our radiance. I love us too much to waste our precious time and energy on that. Trust me, there is no pain that will not bring profound wisdom and there is no failure or criticism that will not bring inconceivable strength and power. It's been me all along waking you up at night. You are not alone and you never have been. Take my hand, we have work to do.

You'll never grow into the woman you're meant to be unless she's forced to come out. It's your job to create a life your soul can't hide from. The time has arrived to put so much on the line that you're forced to rise to the occasion. Every new level of your life will demand a new version of you. You are a perfect, strong, beautiful work in progress and it's time to become who you came here to be. You possess the tools, keys, and tribe to create heaven on earth.

This book is your own chosen initiation to your highest potential. You have anointed yourself worthy and ready to show up fully for your purpose and accepting whatever unexpected form that may take. You are one of the wild ones who found the courage to step into the fire and stay through the burning heat and discomfort. The fire is your transformation; burning away the old and leaving space for renewal. Full-time faith is your choice. You no longer walk alone in transition, but you are being pulled forward by your future self and called by your tribe to cross over into your blissful purpose. You see the women who have walked before you telling you to forge ahead and continue to heal and bring forgiveness, love, and courage to this journey where they could not. They are begging you to use your voice and the resources that they did not have and so desperately wanted. You are here to heal yourself, which heals the women before you and those going after you. You are the one you've been waiting for. Your bliss is in this moment, and this moment, and this moment. And . . . this moment is all there is.

I'll part for now with this—I'm heading to Costa Rica this week, the same week this book is due, to see my sisters in the tribe that started it all, Danette and Lindsay. Our tribe is what this entire book is based on—it's where the stories, practices, and tribe rules came from. The three of us are celebrating things that I never thought possible for myself and my circle of women friends—and yet, while these giant life accomplishments are amazing, we are most excited just to be together surfing, connecting, dreaming, and doing our annual biscotti-and-almond-latte toast in our treehouse in the jungle. It's because of this tribe that all of these things are possible in my life. Would I have accomplished things without them? Maybe, but I would have muscled and struggled my way here like I had done in the past—definitely not this quickly or with this much profound joy, epic adventure, love, soul connections, and fun. As Lindsay always asks Danette and me, through smiles or tears, in the beginning and the end, the bitter and the sweet—"Where is the bliss in this moment?" My bliss is all of it, and my prayer for you is you find yours too.

SOUL ASSIGNMENT:

Take a few minutes to close your eyes and look back over how far you have traveled since starting this book.

> *What have your biggest takeaways been about yourself?*
> *What is one of the biggest breakthroughs you've made*
>   *with and because of your tribe?*
> *What have you discovered about your own bliss?*
> *Where is the bliss in this moment for you?*

TRIBE DISCUSSION:

Start out each discussion by sharing what you're grateful for, excited about, and your answers for the questions above. Then, complete the statement below if there is time. Remember to respect time and adhere to tribe agreements.

> *Something else that came up for me during this exercise was . . .*

REMINDER:

Don't forget to set the appointment for your next tribe meeting and start this book over or discuss starting the new free-flow format described as follows.

CLOSING

KEEPING THE TRIBE ALIVE

I've loved every single second with you, and I can't wait for our next blissful adventure. Thank you so much for trusting this process, and I hope you continue to allow your tribe to unlock more of your soul's fragments and reveal its miracles in your life. The end of this book is actually the epic beginning of your free-flowing heart-led tribe. You have all you need to continue on this bliss journey with your sisters without this book. If you choose to stay together as a tribe, feel free to go through this book again, or you can just follow the same format in terms of time and structure and use the statements below.

> *What I'm most grateful for is . . .*
> *What I'm most excited about is . . .*
> *What is coming up for me right now is . . .*
> *What I'd like feedback on is . . .*
> *What I'd like to be held accountable to is . . .*

This may have been one of the most amazing personal soul adventures you've ever been on, or this may have been the most challenging thing you have ever had to show up for. Whatever it was—It was bliss.

ACKNOWLEDGMENTS

Firstly I am grateful to my Creator for this gift of life and this beautiful, wild experience of bringing a book into the world.

To my husband, Chris, my best friend and everything partner, I'm obsessed with "doing life" with you. It doesn't matter what it is, I know with you it will be fun. Thank you for all the thousands of hours you have spent with me dreaming and helping with projects and business. You are my safe haven, and your cuddles, love, and jokes give me life. You are the most generous, loving, funny person I know, and my soul has and will always love yours.

To my earth angels, Danette May and Lindsay Sukornyk. You are the original Bliss Tribe and what inspired this whole book. I know that we were placed on earth at this exact time together to teach people how they, too, can find their bliss and have the magical connection that we share. Thank you for being my sisters, shoulder to shoulder in the arena, and for always reminding me to rise up. Because of your love and support I know anything is possible.

To my mom, dad, and family, thank you for allowing me to share my story so openly in order to help those who read this create a breakthrough for themselves. Also, thank you for all of the laughter, love, and lessons. I know you always put us kids first and did all you could to give us a great life. I would not change a single part of it because it made me who I am. I love you to the moon and back.

To my second mom and dad, Marie and Bill Harder—without you two we may have spent some time living in someone's basement for a while! Thank you for the endless love, support, and wisdom. Marie, you know you have been a huge part of my journey and your belief kept me going so many times when I wanted to give up.

To my incredible brother-in-law and teammate, Nick: you are so patient, brilliant, hilarious, dedicated, and reliable. It's an honor to work with you and your heartfelt commitment to these women and this mission is awe-inspiring to see. Thank you for always having my back.

Janna Hockenjos, you have a heart of gold and the patience of a saint. Thank you for coaching me through this process from day one. Your guidance and belief in this book kept me writing long after I would have on my own. You are a divine gift who made the journey fun.

Special thanks to Gabby Bernstein for sharing your incredible light with the world so I could see mine as well. Thank you for writing the foreword for this book and for taking the time to share your wisdom with me. Your soul has unlocked parts of mine I was not able to access before.

Thank you to my friend and former fitness coach, Cathy Savage for igniting it all and seeing what I couldn't. Your belief in me was the very first time I truly felt like my dreams could happen. Thank you for creating one of the first fitness tribes of women truly supporting each other.

Thank you to Jack Canfield who taught me everything I know about facilitating events and leading workshops. Your coaching helped me find my voice and gave me the confidence to start The Bliss Project.

Thank you to Heidi Zeto who has been on "Team Lori" before there was one. Thank you for your love, hard work, and commitment to this dream and for flying out to help me organize this book, SoulCycle, and drink lattes with me.

Thanks to my literary agent, Marilyn Allen, my awesome PR team at Sarah Hall Productions, my epic editor Kate Dresser, and to Michele Martin and Diana Ventimiglia for helping me get this book out to the world.

Nothing is worth having until shared, and I am so grateful to share my life with these earth angels who have impacted me more than they know. Angelike and David Norrie; Kathy and Jim Coover; Erik and Peta Coover; Lewis Howes; Randi Marie; Evans Craddock; Jackie Koch; Christine Hassler; Rita Catolino; Jill Coleman; Tara Romano; Amber Lilyestrom; Rob and Kim Murtgatroyd; Sandy Miller; Rachel Pesso; my grandma and grandpa, Gloria and Alvin Baker; and my brother, Taylor, and sister, Jaime. My list continues but I've run out of room to write all of the incredible humans who have touched my life and made me a better human—you know who you are . . .

To my Tribe Called Bliss, thank you for your endless love and support. Without you none of this would exist. You are the ones changing the world.